D1470332

# HOW TO LOOK FOR TROUBLE

*A STRATFOR Guide to Protective Intelligence*

*STRATFOR*
*700 Lavaca Street, Suite 900*
*Austin, Texas 78701*

*Printed in the United States of America*

*The contents of this book originally appeared as analyses*
*on STRATFOR's subscription Web site.*

*ISBN: 1451528205*
*EAN-13: 9781451528206*

*Publisher: Grant Perry*
*Editor: Michael McCullar*
*Project Coordinator: Robert Inks*
*Designer: TJ Lensing*

# CONTENTS

## CHAPTER 3: PROTECTING PEOPLE

## CHAPTER 4: SAFEGUARDING PLACES

# INTRODUCTION

Protective intelligence (PI) is a concept we adopted and refined while working as special agents in the counterterrorism investigations division of the U.S. State Department's Diplomatic Security Service. When agents from our office were dispatched to investigate an incident such as an embassy bombing, assassination or kidnapping, our efforts were focused not only on determining who conducted the attack but also on gathering all the minute details of how the attack was conducted. The idea behind PI, simply enough, is to focus on intelligence that will help prevent the next attack from occurring.

Determining who was responsible for conducting an attack is important, especially if there is to be some sort of military operation directed against the guilty party or an attempt to bring the perpetrator to justice in a court of law. But focusing investigative efforts solely on identifying the perpetrator is not always useful in preventing future attacks and saving lives, which is the goal of PI.

Practitioners of protective intelligence carefully study the tactics, tradecraft and behavior associated with militant actors involved in terrorist attacks, threatening criminals and the mentally disturbed — anyone, really, wanting to do harm to someone else. By understanding how attacks are conducted — i.e., the exact steps and actions required for a successful attack — measures can then be taken to proactively identify early indicators that planning for an attack is under way. Even before it is known who is involved in the activity, the fact that someone is undertaking such efforts can be identified.

This is an important capability in the current terrorist environment, where lone wolves and small cells comprise such a large portion of the threat spectrum. Once such indicators of suspicious behavior are noted, the people involved in planning the attack can then be focused on and identified and action can be taken to prevent them from conducting the attack or attacks they are plotting. Studying the how of an attack also allows one to observe the vulnerabilities in security measures that were exploited by the attackers and permits security measures to be altered accordingly to prevent similar attacks in the future.

PI is based on the fact that attacks don't just happen out of the blue. Most follow a discernible attack cycle in which there are critical points when a plot is most likely to be detected by an outside observer. Two of these points are when surveillance is being conducted and weapons are being acquired. However, there are other, less obvious points when people on the lookout can spot preparations for an attack. It is true that individuals sometimes conduct ill-conceived, poorly executed attacks that involve shortcuts in the planning process, but this type of spur-of-the-moment attack is usually associated with mentally disturbed individuals, and it is extremely rare for a militant actor or professional criminal to conduct a spontaneous terrorist attack without first following the steps of the attack cycle.

To really understand the nuts and bolts of an attack, PI practitioners cannot simply acknowledge that something like surveillance occurs. It is critical to understand exactly how the surveillance is conducted. PI practitioners must turn a powerful lens on attack elements like preoperational surveillance to gain an in-depth understanding of it and all the behaviors and operational elements that go along with the process. Dissecting an activity like preoperational surveillance requires more than simply examining subjects such as the demeanor demonstrated by those conducting surveillance prior to an attack and the specific methods and cover for action and cover for status used. It also requires identifying particular times where surveillance is most likely and the optimal vantage points (called "perches" in surveillance jargon) from where a surveillant is most likely to operate when monitoring a specific facility or event. This type of complex understanding of surveillance can then be used to help focus human or technological countersurveillance efforts where they can be most effective.

Unfortunately, many counterterrorism investigators are so focused on identifying the perpetrator that they do not focus on collecting this type of granular "how" information. Prosecution is the priority instead of prevention. When we have spoken with law enforcement officers responsible for investigating recent grassroots plots, they often have given us blank stares in response to questions about how the suspects conducted surveillance on the intended targets. Too many investigators are not drilling down into specificity regarding surveillance. This is an intelligence failure. Too often, they simply do not pay attention to this type of detail. But this oversight is not really the investigators' fault. No one has ever explained to them why paying attention to, and recording, this type of detail is important.

Moreover, it takes specific training and a practiced eye to observe and record these details without glossing over them. For example, it is quite useful if a protective intelligence officer has first conducted a lot of surveillance, because conducting surveillance allows one to understand what a surveillant must do and where he must be in order to effectively observe a specific person or place.

Militants and criminals conducting attacks and security personnel attempting to guard against such attacks have long engaged in a tactical game of cat and mouse. As militants and criminals adopt new tactics, security measures are then implemented to counter those tactics. The security changes then cause the attackers to change in response and the cycle begins again. However, the basic tools of protective intelligence, once mastered, allow the investigator or analyst to spot trends and shifting paradigms as they develop. This is what allowed STRATFOR to discuss the dangers of al Qaeda in the Arabian Peninsula's innovative bomb designs (and the potential for their employment against aircraft) in September 2009, well before the Christmas Day attack against Northwest Airlines flight 253.

Becoming a seasoned PI practitioner takes years and a lot of practical experience, but almost anyone can take the basic principles of protective intelligence and employ them effectively to spot suspicious behavior. One of the grand secrets we want to share is that when it comes to terrorist and criminal tradecraft, the bad guys are not really as good as the public is led to believe. They are often awkward and make mistakes. One of the big factors that allow them to succeed is that nobody is looking for them. When they are "watched back," the likelihood of their mission succeeding is dramatically reduced.

Scott Stewart, VP, Tactical Intelligence
Fred Burton, VP, Counterterrorism
STRATFOR
Austin, Texas
Feb. 12, 2010

# A NOTE ON CONTENT

STRATFOR presents the following reports as they originally appeared on our subscription Web site, www.STRATFOR.com. These pieces represent some of our best tutorials related to protective intelligence since December 2005, organized under chapter headings and presented in the order in which they were published. Since most of the articles were written as individual analyses, there may be overlap from piece to piece and chapter to chapter, and some of the information may seem dated. Naturally, some observations are linked to a specific time or event years removed from today's security environment, which continues to evolve, but the recommendations and principles are every bit as relevant today as they were when they were written.

# CHAPTER 1: PRINCIPLES AND CHALLENGES

## The Problem of the Lone Wolf
### *May 30, 2007*

Historically, gunmen and bombers who act on their own — lone wolves — have posed a significant threat in the United States. Indeed, from the assassination of President Abraham Lincoln to the slaying of music legend John Lennon they have presented a far more deadly threat to prominent people in the United States than have militant groups. Additionally, as demonstrated by cases such as the 1991 Luby's restaurant shooting in Killeen, Texas, or the recent Virginia Tech massacre, they also pose a grave danger to ordinary Americans.

Due to their often solitary, withdrawn nature, lone wolves present unique problems for security and law enforcement, as their very qualities make it hard for law enforcement or protective security details to gather intelligence regarding their intentions. However, they are not impossible to guard against. Lone wolves frequently take actions in advance of an attack that make them vulnerable to detection by a proactive, protective intelligence program that incorporates investigation and countersurveillance.

Although they most often are male, there is no single profile of the lone wolf. Some are ideologically motivated, some are religiously inspired, some are mentally disturbed, and still others can have a combination of these characteristics. On the ideological side are some leaders (especially among far-right extremists) who promote the concept of "leaderless resistance." This idea perhaps was most widely promulgated by former Klansman Louis Beam. In a February 1992 essay, Beam outlines a plan to over-haul the white supremacist movement — calling for the formation of small, autonomous cells that were to be driven by ideology rather than act under the direction of membership groups. Beam's argu-ment was that this leaderless resistance would have superior opera-tional security and be more successful in conducting attacks than the membership groups, which he believed (correctly) were filled with informants.

In his essay, Beam envisioned a two-tiered approach to the revo-lutionary struggle. One tier would be the above-ground "organs of information," which would "distribute information using newspa-pers, leaflets, computers, etc." The organs of information were not to conduct any illegal activities. The second tier would be made up of individual operators and small "phantom" cells that would conduct attacks. These people were to remain low-key and anonymous, with no traceable connections to the above-ground activists. Beam wrote, "It becomes the responsibility of the individual to acquire the neces-sary skills and information as to what is to be done."

Perhaps one of the most prolific, and least known, ideological lone wolf terrorists was neo-Nazi Joseph Paul Franklin, who conducted a string of arsons and shootings from 1977 to 1980 in an effort to spark a race war in the United States. Franklin, who frequently targeted mixed-race couples, killed at least 20 people during his attacks, which by his own account also included failed assassination attempts against Hustler magazine publisher Larry Flynt and then-National Urban League President Vernon Jordan.

Included in the religious realm are "Phineas Priests," people who believe they have been chosen by God and set apart to act as his "agents of vengeance" on Earth. Phineas Priests frequently conduct attacks against abortion providers and homosexuals — targets they believe have violated biblical law. Phineas Priests derive their name from Phineas, an Old Testament character who killed an Israelite man and a Midianite woman and who was credited with stopping the idolatry brought into the midst of the Israelites by Midianite women. Most Phineas Priests, including Buford Furrow and Eric Rudolph, are adherents to the racist and anti-Semitic Christian Identity religion. Christian Identity, however, does not have a monopoly on religiously motivated lone wolves. Radical Roman Catholics like James Kopp, Protestants such as Paul Hill and Muslims like Mir Amal Kansi and D.C. sniper John Allen Muhammad also have committed religiously motivated attacks.

Though many, if not most, of the ideologically and religiously motivated lone wolves exhibit some degree of mental illness, other mentally ill attackers have no ideological or religious motivation. Some of these individuals "go postal" and commit their attacks at work, while others attack at malls or schools. Unlike the ideological (and even some of the religious) lone wolves, who purposefully choose the leaderless resistance model to thwart law enforcement, the mentally disturbed are generally self-motivated and self-contained.

Lynette "Squeaky" Fromme and Sara Jane Moore, both serving life sentences for attempting to assassinate U.S. President Gerald Ford during separate incidents, are two rare female lone wolves. Fromme, a follower of jailed cult leader Charles Manson, pointed a loaded pistol at Ford in Sacramento, Calif., on Sept. 5, 1975, but was wrestled to the ground by a Secret Service agent before she could fire a shot. Seventeen days later, Moore, an accountant and political radical, fired one shot at Ford after he left the St. Francis Hotel in San Francisco, but missed.

## The Problem for Police

A prime example of the problem lone wolves pose for police is Unabomber Theodore Kaczynski, who began sending improvised explosive devices to random targets in 1978 but was not arrested until 1996. During those 18 years, Kaczynski sent out 16 devices, several of which either did not explode or did not function as designed. Although this allowed authorities to recover a large quantity of physical evidence, Kaczynski's isolation kept him from being identified. It was only after the publication of Kaczynski's "Unabomber Manifesto" in 1995 that his brother came forward to the FBI and identified him as a possible suspect.

When investigating a militant organization it is possible for law enforcement or intelligence agencies to plant informants within the group. Even small, insular groups are vulnerable because it is not uncommon for one or more members of the group to get cold feet and inform authorities about the group's plans to commit acts of violence. With a lone wolf, however, there is no such possibility of infiltration or betrayal. If the suspect never discusses his or her plans with anyone else, he or she can easily fly under law enforcement radar. In most cases, these kinds of individuals can be highly successful in carrying out an attack, especially against vulnerable soft targets.

Mentally disturbed lone wolves pose particular problems because they often have an extremely narrow focus of interest and cannot be diverted to an easier target by heightened security measures. There are some notable exceptions to this, however. For example, Phineas Priest Furrow conducted surveillance on several Jewish targets and bypassed some of them because he considered their security too tight, and neo-Nazi Franklin diverted from the Rev. Jesse Jackson to Jordan after he found Jackson's security to be too robust for his purposes.

Mentally disturbed lone wolves also frequently have an almost total disregard for the consequences of their actions, and quite often show no concern about escaping after they attack, as exemplified by John Hinckley, who did not attempt to flee after attempting to assassinate President Ronald Reagan in 1981. Frequently, as in the case of Virginia Tech shooter Seung-Hui Cho and Luby's shooter George Hennard, the attacker will commit suicide.

When lone wolves do choose to escape and conduct a string of attacks, their anonymous nature and isolation frequently complicates the situation for law enforcement, especially if they take efforts to conceal their identities and minimize the amount of physical evidence they leave. For example, Franklin was able to operate for three years before he was identified and arrested because he spaced his attacks apart in terms of geography and time, and frequently changed his vehicles, weapons and appearance. In fact, it was only after his arrest and confession that the full scope of his activities was realized. Rudolph also traveled great distances between targets and took efforts to alter his appearance.

## The Threat

Because of this history, and the problems specifically posed by lone wolves, local, state and federal law enforcement sources say they are particularly concerned about the threat of individual extremists. This is not exclusively a big-city problem, as several lone wolf incidents have occurred outside of major metropolitan areas, in suburbs or smaller cities. Federal counterterrorism sources, citing the relative ease of attacking in a public place — as demonstrated at Virginia Tech and other locations — have expressed serious concern about the possibility of similar assaults being perpetrated by an Islamist militant or a white supremacist. The logic is that if a mentally disturbed individual can execute such an attack, what prevents an ideologically inspired terrorist from doing the same — or worse?

Because lone wolves are widely dispersed throughout the United States and are distributed across the ideological and social spectrum, it is especially challenging for law enforcement to identify them before they act. The same is true of potential lone wolf extremists. Moreover, it is extremely difficult to differentiate between those extremists who intend to commit attacks from those who simply preach hate or hold radical beliefs (things that are not in themselves illegal). Therefore, authorities must spend a great deal of time and resources looking for individuals who might be moving from radical beliefs to radical actions in an attempt to single out likely lone wolves before they strike. With such a large universe of potential suspects, that is akin to looking for a needle in a haystack.

## Rearing Their Heads

There are some signals that can be watched for in connection with lone wolves. In fact, in retrospect, it is clear that the majority of lone wolves came to the attention of authorities at some point before their attack. Frequently in workplace violence and school shooting cases, the perpetrators are found to have had prior brushes with the law and/or the mental health system. However, attempting to sort lone wolves out from the heavy stream of people who come to the attention of the police and mental health professionals is another difficult search through a very large haystack.

These individuals, though, often frequently exhibit behaviors by which they reveal themselves. Lone wolves, especially mentally disturbed ones, frequently attempt to make written or telephonic contact with their targets before making physical contact. It is at this time that they can be identified and investigated by security or law enforcement personnel. Monitoring the tenor of the contacts from such individuals can also help to indicate their future intentions and provide indications of a deteriorating mental state.

Another sign of a possible lone wolf is when a dedicated and committed extremist suddenly quits a membership group and goes into "radio silence mode." For example, Bob Matthews and three other members "left" the National Alliance in 1983 to form the domestic terrorist group "The Order." In 1999, World Church of the Creator member Benjamin Smith, who had been named "Creator of the Year" for his zeal and dedication, left the group shortly before going on a three-day shooting spree in Illinois and Indiana that randomly targeted racial and ethnic minorities. Smith killed two people and wounded nine others before committing suicide while being chased by police.

Perhaps the most common time that lone wolf assailants self-identify — and the point at which they are most vulnerable to being identified before an attack — is when they are conducting pre-operational surveillance of their potential targets (when they are stalking, in other words). Since pre-operational surveillance involves establishing patterns, potential attackers will stalk their targets several times. Thus, each time they improve the chance they will be observed, especially if the target is employing countersurveillance in search of such threats.

Countersurveillance — the process of detecting and mitigating hostile surveillance — is an important aspect of counterterrorism and security operations. Good countersurveillance is proactive, meaning it provides a means to prevent an attack from happening. This can be a group effort performed by a dedicated countersurveillance team, or it can be done by individuals who simply make the effort to be aware of their surroundings and watch for people or vehicles that seem out of place.

Lone wolves are especially vulnerable to detection during the surveillance phase because they do not have others to assist them. Conducting solo surveillance against a moving target is one of the hardest tasks any professional surveillance operative can be tasked with, and it is even more difficult for an amateur. In a solo surveillance, the operative is forced to reveal himself repeatedly over time and distance, and in different environments. Also, a person unskilled in the art of surveillance, especially one who is mentally disturbed, will frequently commit many errors of demeanor. Thus, their odd behavior and crude surveillance technique — they frequently stalk and lurk — make them easy to pick out.

Because of this, countersurveillance — whether by law enforcement, intelligence agencies, corporations or individuals — is a critical means of spotting lone wolves during the target selection and planning stage, the time the operation is most vulnerable to detection and interdiction. It is important to be able to recognize hostile surveillance by a lone wolf before the next phase of the attack cycle begins, for once the actual attack is in progress, it cannot be undone.

# The Secrets of Countersurveillance
## *June 6, 2007*

Almost any criminal act, from a purse-snatching to a terrorist bombing, involves some degree of pre-operational surveillance. In fact, one common denominator of all the different potential threats — whether from lone wolves, militant groups, common criminals or the mentally disturbed — is that those planning an operation all monitor their target in advance. However, while pickpockets or purse-snatchers case their victims for perhaps only a few seconds or minutes, a militant organization might conduct detailed surveillance of a target for several weeks or even months.

Regardless of the length of time surveillance is performed, however, the criminal or militant conducting it is exposed and therefore vulnerable to detection. Because of this, countersurveillance (CS) — the process of detecting and mitigating hostile surveillance — is an important, though often overlooked, element of counterterrorism and security operations. CS is especially important because it is one of the few security measures that allows for threats to be dealt with before they can develop into active attacks.

An effective CS program depends on knowing two "secrets": first, hostile surveillance is vulnerable to detection because those performing it are not always as sophisticated in their tradecraft as commonly perceived; and second, hostile surveillance can be manipulated and the operatives forced into making errors that will reveal their presence.

## The First Secret

Various potential assailants use different attack cycles, which vary depending on the nature and objectives of the plotter. For example, the typical six-step terrorist attack cycle does not always apply to a suicide bomber (who is not concerned about escape) or a mentally disturbed stalker (who is not concerned about escape or media exploitation). It is during the early phases of the attack cycle — the target selection and the planning phases — that the plotters conduct their surveillance, though they can use a surveillance team even during the actual attack to signal that the target is approaching the attack zone.

The purpose of pre-operational surveillance is to determine the target's vulnerabilities. Surveillance helps quantify the target, note possible weaknesses and begin to identify potential attack methods. When the target is a person, perhaps targeted for assassination or kidnapping, surveillants will look for patterns of behavior such as the time the target leaves for work, the transportation method and the route taken. They also will take note of the type of security, if any, the target uses. For fixed targets such as buildings, the surveillance will be used to determine physical security measures as well as patterns of behavior within the guard force, if guards are employed. For example, the plotters will look not only for fences, gates, locks and alarms but also for times when fewer guards are present or when the guards are about to come on or off their shifts. All of this information will then be used to select the best time and location for the attack, the type of attack and the resources needed to execute it.

Since an important objective of pre-operational surveillance is establishing patterns, the operatives will conduct their surveillance several times, often at different times of the day. Additionally, they will follow a mobile target to different environments and in diverse locations. This is when it is important to know the first "secret" of CS: surveillants are vulnerable to detection. In fact, the more surveillance they conduct the greater the chances are that they will be observed. Once that happens, security personnel can be alerted and the entire plan compromised. Additionally, surveillants who themselves are being watched can unwittingly lead intelligence and law enforcement agencies to other members of their organization.

## Surveillance

A large and professional surveillance team can use a variety of fixed and mobile assets, including electronic listening devices and operatives on foot, in vehicles and even in aircraft. Such a large team can be extremely difficult for anyone to spot. A massive surveillance operation, however, requires an organization with vast assets and a large number of well-trained operatives. This level of surveillance, therefore, is usually only found at the governmental level, as most militant organizations lack the assets and the number of trained personnel required to mount such an operation. Indeed, most criminal and militant surveillance is conducted by one person, or by a small group of operatives. This means they must place themselves in a position to see the target — and thus be seen — with far more frequency than would be required in a huge surveillance operation. And the more they show their faces, the more vulnerable they are to detection. This vulnerability is amplified if the operatives are not highly trained.

The al Qaeda manual "Military Studies in the Jihad Against the Tyrants" and its online training magazines not only instruct operatives planning an attack to conduct surveillance, they also point out the type of information that should be gathered. These documents, however, do not teach jihadist operatives how to go about gathering the required information. In the United States, the Ruckus Society's Scouting Manual provides detailed instructions for conducting surveillance, or "scouting," as the society calls it, on "direct action" targets. Following written instructions, however, does not automatically translate into having skilled surveillance operatives on the street. This is because, while some basic skills and concepts can be learned by reading, applying that information to a real-world situation, particularly in a hostile environment, can be exceedingly difficult. This is especially true when the application requires subtle and complex skills that are difficult to master.

The behaviors necessary to master surveillance tradecraft are not intuitive and in fact frequently run counter to human nature. Because of this, intelligence and security professionals who work surveillance operations receive in-depth training that includes many hours of heavily critiqued practical exercises, often followed by field training with experienced surveillance operatives.

Most militant groups do not provide this level of training, and poor tradecraft has long proved to be an Achilles' heel for militants, who typically use a small number of poorly trained operatives to conduct their surveillance operations.

What does "bad" surveillance look like? The U.S. government uses the acronym TEDD to illustrate the principles one can use to identify surveillance. A person who sees someone repeatedly over Time, in different Environments, over Distance or who displays poor Demeanor can assume he or she is under surveillance. Surveillants who exhibit poor demeanor, meaning they act unnaturally, can look blatantly suspicious, though they also can be lurkers — those who have no reason for being where they are or for doing what they are doing. Sometimes they exhibit almost imperceptible behaviors that the target senses more than observes. Other giveaways include moving when the target moves, communicating when the target moves, avoiding eye contact with the target, making sudden turns or stops, or even using hand signals to communicate with other members of a surveillance team.

The mistakes made while conducting surveillance can be quite easy to catch — as long as someone is looking for them. If no one is looking, however, hostile surveillance is remarkably easy. This is why militant groups have been able to get away with conducting surveillance for so long using bumbling operatives who practice poor tradecraft.

## The Second Secret

At the most basic level, CS can be performed by a person who is aware of his or her surroundings and who is watching for people who violate the principles of TEDD. At a more advanced level, the single person can use surveillance detection routes (SDRs) to draw out surveillance. This leads to the second "secret": Due to the nature of surveillance, those conducting it can be manipulated and forced to tip their hand.

It is far more difficult to surveil a mobile target than a stationary one, and an SDR is a tool that takes advantage of this difficulty and uses a carefully designed route to flush out surveillance. The SDR is intended to look innocuous from the outside, but it is cleverly calculated to evoke certain behaviors from the surveillant.

When members of a highly trained surveillance team recognize that the person they are following is executing an SDR — and therefore is trying to manipulate them — they will frequently take countermeasures suitable to the situation and their mission. This can include dropping off the target and picking up surveillance another day, bypassing the channel, stair-step or other trap the target is using and picking him or her up at another location along their projected route. It can even include "bumper locking" the target or switching to a very overt mode of surveillance to let the target know that his SDR was detected — and not appreciated. Untrained surveillants who have never encountered an SDR, however, frequently can be sucked blindly into such traps.

Though intelligence officers performing an SDR need to look normal from the outside — in effect appear as if they are not running an SDR — people who are acting protectively on their own behalf have no need to be concerned about being perceived as being "provocative" in their surveillance detection efforts. They can use very aggressive elements of the SDR to rapidly determine whether the surveillance they suspect does in fact exist — and if it does, move rapidly to a preselected safe-haven.

At a more advanced level is the dedicated CS team, which can be deployed to determine whether a person or facility is under surveillance. This team can use mobile assets, fixed assets or a combination of both. The CS team is essentially tasked to watch for watchers. To do this, team members identify places — "perches," in surveillance jargon — that an operative would need to occupy in order to surveil a potential target. They then watch those perches for signs of hostile surveillance.

CS teams can manipulate surveillance by "heating up" particular perches with static guards or roving patrols, thus forcing the surveillants away from those areas and toward another perch or perches where the CS team can then focus its detection efforts. They also can use overt, uniformed police or guards to stop, question and identify any suspicious person they observe. This can be a particularly effective tactic, as it can cause militants to conclude that the facility they are monitoring is too difficult to attack. Even if the security forces never realized the person was actually conducting surveillance, such an encounter normally will lead the surveillant to assume that he or she has been identified and that the people who stopped him knew exactly what he was doing.

Confrontational techniques can stop a hostile operation dead in its tracks and cause the operatives to focus their hostile efforts elsewhere. These techniques include overt field interviews, overt photography of suspected hostiles, and the highly under-utilized "Terry stop," in which a law enforcement officer in the United States can legally stop, interview and frisk a person for weapons if the officer has a reasonable suspicion that criminal activity is afoot, even if the officer's suspicions do not rise to the level of making an arrest.

Also, by denying surveillants perches that are close to the target's point of origin or destination (home or work, for example), a CS team can effectively push hostile surveillance farther and farther away. This injects a great deal of ambiguity into the situation and complicates the hostile information-collection effort. For instance, if surveillants do not know what car the target drives, they can easily obtain that information by sitting outside of the person's home and watching what comes out of the garage or driveway. By contrast, surveillants forced to use a perch a mile down the road might have dozens of cars to choose from. A CS team also can conduct more sophisticated SDRs than a lone individual.

In addition, the CS team will keep detailed logs of the people and vehicles it encounters and will database this information along with photos of possible hostiles. This database allows the team to determine whether it has encountered the same person or vehicle repeatedly on different shifts or at different sites. This analytical component of the CS team is essential to the success of the team's efforts, especially when there are multiple shifts working the CS operation or multiple sites are being covered. People also have perishable memories, and databasing ensures that critical information is retained and readily retrievable.

Although professional CS teams normally operate in a low-key fashion in order to collect information without changing the behaviors of suspected hostiles, there are exceptions to this rule. When the team believes an attack is imminent, for example, or when the risk of allowing a hostile operation to continue undisturbed is unacceptable, team members are likely to break cover and confront hostile surveillants. In cases like these, CS teams have the advantage of surprise. Indeed, materializing out of nowhere to confront the suspected surveillant can be more effective than the arrival of overt security assets.

Well-trained CS teams have an entire arsenal of tricks at their disposal to manipulate and expose hostile surveillance. In this way, they can proactively identify threats early in the attack cycle — and possibly prevent attacks.

---

## Threats, Situational Awareness and Perspective
*Aug. 22, 2007*

In last week's Terrorism Intelligence Report, we said U.S. counterterrorism sources remain concerned an attack will occur on U.S. soil in the next few weeks. Although we are skeptical of these reports, al Qaeda and other jihadists do retain the ability — and the burning desire — to conduct tactical strikes within the United States. One thing we did not say last week, however, was that we publish such reports not to frighten readers, but to impress upon them the need for preparedness, which does not mean paranoia.

Fear and paranoia, in fact, are counterproductive to good personal and national security, and we have tried over the past few years to place what we consider hyped threats into the proper perspective. To this end, we have addressed threats such as al Qaeda's chemical and biological weapons capabilities, reports of a looming "American

Hiroshima" nuclear attack against the United States, the dirty-bomb threat, the smoky-bomb threat, and the threat of so-called "mubtakkar devices," among others.

Though some threats are indeed hyped, the world nonetheless remains a dangerous place. Undoubtedly, at this very moment, some people are seeking ways to carry out attacks against targets in the United States. Moreover, terrorism attacks are not the only threat — far more people are victimized by common criminals. Does this reality mean that people need to live in constant fear and paranoia? Not at all. If people do live that way, those who seek to terrorize them have won. However, by taking a few relatively simple precautions and adjusting their mindsets, people can live less-stressful lives during these uncertain times. One of the keys to personal preparedness and protection is to have a contingency plan in place in the event of an attack or other major emergency. The second element is practicing situational awareness.

## The Proper State of Mind

Situational awareness is the process of recognizing a threat at an early stage and taking measures to avoid it. Being observant of one's surroundings and identifying potential threats and dangerous situations is more of an attitude or mindset than it is a hard skill. Because of this, situational awareness is not just a process that can be practiced by highly trained government agents or specialized corporate security countersurveillance teams — it can be adopted and employed by anyone.

An important element of this mindset is first coming to the realization that a threat exists. Ignorance or denial of a threat — or completely tuning out one's surroundings while in a public place — makes a person's chances of quickly recognizing the threat and avoiding it slim to none. This is why apathy, denial and complacency are so deadly.

An example is the case of Terry Anderson, the Associated Press bureau chief in Lebanon who was kidnapped on March 16, 1985.

15

The day before his abduction, Anderson was driving in Beirut traffic when a car pulled in front of his and nearly blocked him in. Due to the traffic situation, and undoubtedly a bit of luck, Anderson was able to avoid what he thought was an automobile accident — even though events like these can be hallmarks of pre-operational planning. The next day, Anderson's luck ran out as the same vehicle successfully blocked his vehicle in the same spot. Anderson was pulled from his vehicle at gunpoint — and held hostage for six years and nine months.

Clearly, few of us are living in the type of civil war conditions that Anderson faced in 1985 Beirut. Nonetheless, average citizens face all kinds of threats today — from common thieves and assailants to criminals and mentally disturbed individuals who want to conduct violent acts to militants aiming to carry out large-scale attacks. Should an attack occur, then, a person with a complacent or apathetic mindset will be taken completely by surprise and could freeze up in shock and denial as his or her mind is forced to quickly adjust to a newly recognized and unforeseen situational reality. That person is in no condition to react, flee or resist.

Denial and complacency, however, are not the only hazardous states of mind. As mentioned above, paranoia and obsessive concern about one's safety and security can be just as dangerous. There are times when it is important to be on heightened alert — a woman walking alone in a dark parking lot is one example — but people are simply not designed to operate in a state of heightened awareness for extended periods of time. The body's "flight or fight" response is helpful in a sudden emergency, but a constant stream of adrenalin and stress leads to mental and physical burnout. It is very hard for people to be aware of their surroundings when they are completely fried.

Situational awareness, then, is best practiced at a balanced level referred to as "relaxed awareness," a state of mind that can be maintained indefinitely without all the stress associated with being on constant alert. Relaxed awareness is not tiring, and allows people to enjoy life while paying attention to their surroundings.

When people are in a state of relaxed awareness, it is far easier to make the transition to a state of heightened awareness than it is to jump all the way from complacency to heightened awareness. So, if something out of the ordinary occurs, those practicing relaxed awareness can heighten their awareness while they attempt to determine whether the anomaly is indeed a threat. If it is, they can take action to avoid it; if it is not, they can stand down and return to a state of relaxed awareness.

## The Telltale Signs

What are we looking for while we are in a state of relaxed awareness? Essentially the same things we discussed when we described what bad surveillance looks like. It is important to remember that almost every criminal act, from a purse-snatching to a terrorist bombing, involves some degree of pre-operational surveillance and that criminals are vulnerable to detection during that time. This is because criminals, even militants planning terrorist attacks, often are quite sloppy when they are casing their intended targets. They have been able to get away with their sloppy practices for so long because most people simply do not look for them. On the positive side, however, that also means that people who are looking can spot them fairly easily.

The U.S. government uses the acronym TEDD to illustrate the principles one can use to identify surveillance, but these same principles also can be used to identify criminal threats. TEDD stands for Time, Environment, Distance and Demeanor. In other words, if a person sees someone repeatedly over time, in different environments and over distance, or one who displays poor demeanor, then that person can assume he or she is under surveillance. If a person is the specific target of a planned attack, he or she might be exposed to the time, environment and distance elements of TEDD, but if the subway car the person is riding in or the building where the person works is the target, he or she might only have the element of demeanor to key on. This also is true in the case of criminals who behave like "ambush predators" and lurk in an area waiting for a victim. Because their attack cycle is extremely condensed, the most important element to watch for is demeanor.

By poor demeanor, we simply mean a person is acting unnaturally. This behavior can look blatantly suspicious, such as someone who is lurking and/or has no reason for being where he is or for doing what he is doing. Sometimes, however, poor demeanor can be more subtle, encompassing almost imperceptible behaviors that the target senses more than observes. Other giveaways include moving when the target moves, communicating when the target moves, avoiding eye contact with the target, making sudden turns or stops, or even using hand signals to communicate with other members of a surveillance team.

In the terrorism realm, exhibiting poor demeanor also can include wearing unseasonably warm clothing, such as trench coats in the summer; displaying odd bulges under clothing or wires protruding from clothing; unnaturally sweating, mumbling or fidgeting; or attempting to avoid security personnel. In addition, according to some reports, suicide bombers often exhibit an intense stare as they approach the final stages of their mission. They seem to have tunnel vision, being able to focus only on their intended target.

## Perspective

We have seen no hard intelligence that supports the assertions that a jihadist attack will occur in the next few weeks and are somewhat skeptical about such reports. Regardless of whether our U.S. counterterrorism sources are correct this time, though, the world remains a dangerous place. Al Qaeda, grassroots jihadists and domestic militants of several different political persuasions have the desire and capability to conduct attacks. Meanwhile, criminals and mentally disturbed individuals, such as the Virginia Tech shooter, appear to be getting more violent every day.

In the big picture, violence and terrorism have always been a part of the human condition. The Chinese built the Great Wall for a reason other than tourism. Today's "terrorists" are far less dangerous to society as a whole than were the Viking berserkers and barbarian tribes who terrorized Europe for centuries, and the ragtag collection of men who have sworn allegiance to Osama bin Laden pose far less of a threat to Western civilization than the large, battle-hardened army Abdul Rahman al-Ghafiqi led into the heart of France in 732.

Terrorist attacks are designed to have a psychological impact that far outweighs the actual physical damage caused by the attack itself. Denying the perpetrators this multiplication effect — as the British did after the July 2005 subway bombings — prevents them from accomplishing their greater goals. Therefore, people should prepare, plan and practice relaxed awareness — and not let paranoia and the fear of terrorism and crime rob them of the joy of life.

---

## Intelligence as a Proactive Tool
### Nov. 7, 2007

On Nov. 4, 46-year-old Spanish businessman Edelmiro Manuel Pérez Merelles was freed from captivity after being held for nearly two weeks by kidnappers who grabbed him from his vehicle in the Mexico City metropolitan area. The fact that a kidnapping occurred in Mexico is not at all unusual. What is unusual is the enormous press coverage the case received, largely because of the audacity and brutality of the attackers.

Pérez Merelles was snatched from his car Oct. 22 after a gang of heavily armed assailants blocked his vehicle and, in full view of witnesses, killed his bodyguard/driver, delivering a coup de grace shot to the back of his head. The abductors then shoved the driver's body into the trunk of Pérez Merelles' car, which was later found abandoned. After the abduction, when the family balked at the exorbitant amount of ransom demanded by the kidnappers, the criminals reportedly upped the ante by sending two of Pérez Merelles' fingers to his family. A ransom finally was paid and Pérez Merelles was released in good health, though sans the fingers.

In a world in which militants and criminals appear increasingly sophisticated and brutal, this case highlights the need for protective intelligence (PI) to augment traditional security measures.

## Action vs. Reaction

As any football player knows, action is always faster than reaction. That principle provides offensive players with a slight edge over their opponents on the defense, because the offensive players know the snap count that will signal the beginning of the play. Now, some crafty defensive players will anticipate or jump the snap to get an advantage over the offensive players, but that anticipation is an action in itself and not a true reaction. This same principle of action and reaction is applicable to security operations. For example, when members of an abduction team launch an assault against a target's vehicle, they have the advantage of tactical surprise over the target and any security personnel protecting the target. This advantage can be magnified significantly if the target lacks the proper mindset and freezes in response to the attack.

Even highly trained security officers who have been schooled in attack recognition and in responding under pressure to attacks against their principal are at a disadvantage once an attack is launched. This is because, in addition to having the element of tactical surprise, the assailants also have conducted surveillance and have planned their attack. Therefore, they presumably have come prepared — with the number of assailants and the right weaponry — to overcome any security assets in place. Simply put, the criminals will not attack unless they believe they have the advantage. Not all attacks succeed, of course. Sometimes the attackers will botch the attempt, and sometimes security personnel are good enough — or lucky enough — to regain the initiative and fight off the attack or otherwise escape. In general, however, once an attack is launched, the attackers have the advantage over the defender, who not only is reacting, but also is simultaneously attempting to identify the source, location and direction of the attack and assess the number of assailants and their armament.

Furthermore, if a gang is brazen enough to conduct a serious crime such as kidnapping for ransom, which carries stiff penalties in most countries, chances are the same group is capable of committing homicide during the crime. So, using the kidnapping example, the gang will account for the presence of any security officers in its planning and will devise a way to neutralize those officers — as the attackers neutralized the bodyguard in the Pérez Merelles abduction.

Even if the target is traveling in an armored vehicle, the attackers will plan a way to immobilize it, breach the armor and get to their victim. In a kidnapping scenario, once the target's vehicle is stopped or disabled, the assailants can place an explosive device on top of it, forcing the occupants to open the door or risk death — a tactic witnessed several times in Latin America — or, if given enough time, they can use hand tools to pry it open like a can of sardines. Since most armored vehicles use the car's factory-installed door-lock system, techniques used by car thieves, such as using master keys or punching out the locks, also can be used effectively against an immobilized armored vehicle.

This same principle applies to physical security measures at buildings. Measures such as badge readers, closed-circuit television coverage, metal detectors, cipher locks and so forth are an important part of any security plan — though they have finite utility. In many cases, assailants have mapped out, quantified and then defeated or bypassed physical security devices, which require human interaction and a proactive security program to optimize their effectiveness.

Armed guards, armored vehicles and physical security devices can all be valuable tools, but they can be defeated by attackers who have planned an attack and then put it into play at the time and place of their choosing. Clearly, a way is needed to deny attackers the advantage of striking when and where they choose or, even better, to stop an attack before it can be launched. In other words, security officers must play on the action side of the action/reaction equation. That is where PI comes in.

## Protective Intelligence

In simple terms, PI is the process used to identify and assess threats. A well-designed PI program will have a number of distinct and crucial components or functions, but the most important of these are countersurveillance, investigations and analysis. The first function, countersurveillance, serves as the eyes and ears of the PI team. As noted above, kidnapping gangs conduct extensive pre-operational surveillance. But all criminals — stalkers, thieves, lone wolves, militant groups, etc. — engage in some degree of pre-operational surveillance, though the length of this surveillance will vary depending on the actor and the circumstances. A purse-snatcher might case a potential target for a few seconds, while a kidnapping gang might conduct surveillance of a potential target for weeks. The degree of surveillance tradecraft — from very clumsy to highly sophisticated — also will vary widely, depending on the operatives' training and street skills.

It is while conducting this surveillance that someone with hostile intentions is most apt to be detected, making this the point in the attack cycle that potential violence can most easily be disrupted or prevented. This is what makes countersurveillance such a valuable proactive tool.

Although countersurveillance teams are valuable, they cannot operate in a vacuum. They need to be part of a larger PI program that includes the analytical and investigative functions. Investigations and analysis are two closely related yet distinct components that can help to focus the countersurveillance operations on the most likely or most vulnerable targets, interpret the observations and identify and track suspicious individuals.

Without an analytical function, it is difficult for countersurveillance operatives to note when the same person or vehicle has been encountered on different shifts or at different sites. In fact, countersurveillance operations are far less valuable when they are conducted without databasing or analyzing what the countersurveillance teams observe over time and distance. Investigations are equally important. Most often, something that appears unusual to a countersurveillance operative has a logical and harmless explanation, though it is difficult to make that determination without an investigative unit to follow-up on red flags.

The investigative and analytical functions also are crucial in assessing communications from mentally disturbed individuals, for tracking the activities of activist or extremist groups and for attempting to identify and assess individuals who make anonymous threats via telephone or mail. Mentally disturbed individuals have long posed a substantial (and still underestimated) threat to both prominent people and average citizens in the United States. In fact, mentally disturbed individuals have killed far more prominent people (including President James Garfield, Bobby Kennedy and John Lennon) than militants have in terrorist attacks. Furthermore, nearly all of those who have committed attacks have self-identified or otherwise come to the attention of authorities before the attack was carried out. Because of this, PI teams ensure that no mentally disturbed person is summarily dismissed as a "harmless nut" until he or she has been thoroughly investigated and his or her communications carefully analyzed and databased. Databasing is crucial because it allows the tenor of correspondence from a mentally disturbed individual to be monitored over time and compared with earlier missives in order to identify signs of a deteriorating mental state or a developing intent to commit violence. PI teams will often consult mental health professionals in such cases to assist with psycholinguistic and psychological evaluations.

Not all threats from the mentally disturbed come from outside a company or organization, however. Although the common perception following a workplace incident is that the employee "just snapped," in most cases the factors leading to the violent outburst have been building up for a long time and the assailant has made detailed plans. Because of this, workplace or school shootings seldom occur randomly. In most cases, the perpetrator has targeted a specific individual or set of individuals that the shooter believes is responsible for his plight. Therefore, PI teams also will work closely with human-resource managers and employee mental health programs to try to identify early on those employees who have the potential to commit acts of workplace violence.

In workplace settings as well as other potential threat areas, PI operatives also can aid other security officers by providing them with photographs and descriptions of any person identified as a potential problem. The person identified as the potential target also can be briefed and the information shared with that person's administrative assistants, family members and household staff.

Another crucial function of a PI team is to "red team," or to look at the security program from the outside and help identify vulnerabilities. Most security looks from the inside out, but PI provides the ability to look from the outside in. In the executive protection realm, this can include an analysis of the principal's schedule and transportation routes in order to determine the most vulnerable times and places. Countersurveillance or even overt security assets can then be focused on these crucial locations.

Red teams also sometimes perform cyberstalker research. That is, they study a potential target through a criminal or mentally disturbed person's eyes — attempting to obtain as much open-source and public record information on that target as possible in order to begin a surveillance operation. Such a project helps determine what sensitive information is available regarding a particular target and highlights how that information could be used by a criminal planning an attack.

Red teams also will attempt to invade a facility in order to test access control or to conduct surveillance on the operations in an effort to identify vantage points (or "perches") that would most likely be used by someone surveilling the facility. Once the perches around one's facility are identified, activities at those sites can be monitored, making it more difficult for assailants to conduct pre-operational surveillance at will.

One other advantage to PI operations is that, being amorphous by nature, they are far more difficult for a potential assailant to detect than are traditional security measures. Even if one PI operative is detected — regardless of whether the team has identified its targets — the surveillers' anxiety will increase because they likely will not know whether the person they encounter is a countersurveillance operative.

This combination of countersurveillance, analysis and investigation can be applied in a number of other creative and proactive ways to help keep potentially threatening people off balance and deny them the opportunity to take the initiative. Although a large global corporation or government might require a large PI team, these core functions can be performed by a skilled, compact team, or even by one person. For example, a person living in a high-threat environment such as Mexico City can acquire the skills to perform his or her own analysis of route and schedule, and can run surveillance detection routes in order to smoke out hostile operations.

The details of the Pérez Merelles kidnapping indicate that it was professionally planned and well-executed. Crimes of this caliber do not occur on the spur of the moment. They require extensive surveillance, intelligence gathering and planning — the very types of activities that are vulnerable to detection through the proactive tool of PI.

---

## Counterterrorism Funding: Old Fears and Cyclical Lulls
*March 18, 2009*

Two years ago, we wrote an article discussing the historical pattern of the boom and bust in counterterrorism spending. In that article we discussed the phenomenon whereby a successful terrorist attack creates a profound shock that is quite often followed by an extended lull. We noted how this dynamic tends to create a pendulum effect in public perception and how public opinion is ultimately translated into public policy that produces security and counterterrorism funding.

In other words, the shock of a successful terrorist attack creates a crisis environment in which the public demands action from the government and Washington responds by earmarking vast amounts of funds to address the problem. Then the lull sets in, and some of the programs created during the crisis are scrapped entirely or are killed by a series of budget cuts as the public's perception of the threat changes and its demands for government action focus elsewhere. The lull eventually is shattered by another attack — and another infusion of money goes to address the now-neglected problem.

On March 13, The Washington Post carried a story entitled "Hardened U.S. Embassies Symbolic of Old Fears, Critics Say." The story discussed the new generation of U.S. Embassy buildings, which are often referred to as "Inman buildings" by State Department insiders. This name refers to buildings constructed in accordance with the physical security standards set by the Secretary of State's Advisory Panel on Overseas Security, a panel chaired by former Deputy CIA Director Adm. Bobby Inman following the 1983 attacks against the U.S. embassies in Beirut and Kuwait City. The 1985 Inman report, which established these security requirements and contributed to one of the historical security spending booms, was also responsible for beefing up the State Department's Office of Security and transforming it into the Diplomatic Security Service (DSS).

It has been 11 years since a U.S. Embassy has been reduced to a smoking hole in the ground, and the public's perception of the threat appears to be changing once again. In The Washington Post article, Stephen Schlesinger, an adjunct fellow at the Century Foundation, faults the new Inman building that serves as the U.S. Mission to the United Nations in New York for being unattractive and uninviting. Schlesinger is quoted as saying: "Rather than being an approachable, beckoning embassy — emphasizing America's desire to open up to the rest of the globe and convey our historically optimistic and progressive values — it sits across from the U.N. headquarters like a dark, forbidding fortress, saying, 'Go away.'" When opinion leaders begin to express such sentiments in The Washington Post, it is an indication that we are now in the lull period of the counterterrorism cycle.

## Tensions Over Security

There has always been a tension between security and diplomacy in the U.S. State Department. There are some diplomats who consider security to be antithetical to diplomacy and, like Mr. Schlesinger, believe that U.S. diplomatic facilities need to be open and accessible rather than secure. These foreign service officers (FSOs) also believe that regional security officers are too risk averse and that they place too many restrictions on diplomats to allow them to practice effective diplomacy. (Regional security officer — RSO — is the title given to a DSS special agent in charge of security at an embassy.) To quote one FSO, DSS special agents are "cop-like morons." People who carry guns instead of demarches and who go out and arrest people for passport and visa fraud are simply not considered "diplomatic." There is also the thorny issue that in their counterintelligence role, DSS agents are often forced to confront FSOs over personal behavior (such as sexual proclivities or even crimes) that could be considered grounds for blackmail by a hostile intelligence service.

On the other side of the coin, DSS agents feel the animosity emanating from those in the foreign service establishment who are hostile to security and who oppose the DSS efforts to improve security at diplomatic missions overseas. DSS agents refer to these FSOs as "black dragons" — a phrase commonly uttered in conjunction with a curse. DSS agents see themselves as the ones left holding the bag when an FSO disregards security guidelines, does something reckless, and is robbed, raped or murdered. It is most often the RSO and his staff who are responsible for going out and picking up the pieces when something turns bad. It is also the RSO who is called before a U.S. government accountability review board when an embassy is attacked and destroyed. In the eyes of a DSS special agent, then, a strong, well-protected building conveys a far better representation of American values and strength than does a smoldering hole in the ground, where an "accessible" embassy once stood. In the mind of a DSS agent, dead diplomats can conduct no diplomacy.

This internal tension has also played a role in the funding boom and bust for diplomatic security overseas. Indeed, DSS agents are convinced that the black dragons consistently attempt to cut security budgets during the lull periods. When career foreign service officers like Sheldon Krys and Anthony Quainton were appointed to serve as assistant secretaries for diplomatic security — and presided over large cuts in budgets and manpower — many DSS agents were convinced that Krys and Quainton had been placed in that position specifically to sabotage the agency.

DSS agents were suspicious of Quainton, in particular, because of his history. In February 1992, while Quainton was serving as the U.S. ambassador to Peru, the ambassador's residence in Lima was attacked by Shining Path guerrillas who detonated a large vehicular-borne improvised explosive device in the street next to it. A team sent by the DSS counterterrorism investigations division to investigate the attack concluded in its report that Quainton's refusal to follow the RSO's recommendation to alter his schedule was partially responsible for the attack. The report angered Quainton, who became the assistant secretary for diplomatic security seven months later. Shortly after assuming his post, Quainton proclaimed to his staff that "terrorism is dead" and ordered the abolishment of the DSS counterterrorism investigations division.

Using a little bureaucratic sleight of hand, then-DSS Director Clark Dittmer renamed the office the Protective Intelligence Investigations Division (PII) and allowed it to maintain its staff and function. Although Quainton had declared terrorism dead, special agents assigned to the PII office would be involved in the investigation of the first known al Qaeda attacks against U.S. interests in Aden and Sanaa, Yemen, in December 1992. They also played a significant role in the investigation of the World Trade Center bombing in February 1993, the investigation of the 1993 New York Landmarks Plot and many subsequent terrorism cases.

## Boom-and-Bust Funding

One of the problems created by the feast-or-famine cycle of security funding is that during the boom times, when there is a sudden (and often huge) influx of cash, agencies sometimes have difficulty spending all the money allotted to them in a logical and productive manner. Congress, acting on strong public opinion, often will give an agency even more than it initially requested for a particular program — and then expect an immediate solution to the problem. Rather than risk losing these funds, the agencies scramble to find ways to spend them. Then, quite often, by the time the agency is able to get its act together and develop a system to effectively use the funds, the lull has set in and funding is cut. These cuts frequently are accompanied by criticism of how the agency spent the initial glut of funding.

Whether or not it was a conscious effort on the part of people like Quainton, funding for diplomatic security programs was greatly reduced during the lull period of the 1990s. In addition to a reduction in the funding provided to build new embassies or bring existing buildings up to Inman standards, RSOs were forced to make repeated cuts in budgets for items such as local guard forces, residential security and the maintenance of security equipment such as closed-circuit television cameras and vehicular barriers.

These budget cuts were identified as a contributing factor in the 1998 bombings of the U.S. embassies in Nairobi and Dar es Salaam. The final report of the Crowe Commission, which was established to investigate the attacks, notes that its accountability review board members "were especially disturbed by the collective failure of the U.S. government over the past decade to provide adequate resources to reduce the vulnerability of U.S. diplomatic missions to terrorist attacks in most countries around the world."

The U.S. Embassy in Nairobi was known to be vulnerable. Following the August 1997 raid on the Nairobi residence of Wadih el-Hage, U.S. officials learned that el-Hage and his confederates had conducted extensive pre-operational surveillance against the U.S. Embassy in Nairobi, indicating that they planned to attack the facility. The U.S. ambassador in Nairobi, citing the embassy's vulnerability to car bomb attacks, asked the state department in December 1997 to authorize a relocation of the embassy to a safer place. In its January 1998 denial of the request, the state department said that, in spite of the threat and vulnerability, the post's "medium" terrorism threat level did not warrant the expenditure.

## Old Fears

The 1998 East Africa embassy bombings highlighted the consequences of the security budget cuts that came during the lull years. Clearly, terrorism was not dead then, nor is it dead today, in spite of the implications in the March 13 Washington Post article. Indeed, the current threat of attacks directed against U.S. diplomatic facilities is very real. Since January 2008, we have seen attacks against U.S. diplomatic facilities in Sanaa, Yemen; Istanbul, Turkey; Kabul, Afghanistan; Belgrade, Serbia; and Monterrey, Mexico (as well as attacks against American diplomats in Pakistan, Sudan and Lebanon). Since 2001, there have also been serious attacks against U.S. diplomatic facilities in Jeddah, Saudi Arabia; Karachi, Pakistan; Damascus, Syria; Athens, Greece; and Baghdad, Iraq.

Even if one believes, as we do, that al Qaeda's abilities have been severely degraded since 9/11, it must be recognized that the group and its regional franchises still retain the ability to conduct tactical strikes. In fact, due to the increased level of security at U.S. diplomatic missions, most of the attacks conducted by jihadists have been directed against softer targets such as hotels or the embassies of other foreign countries. Indeed, attacks that were intended to be substantial strikes against U.S. diplomatic facilities in places like Sanaa, Jeddah and Istanbul have been thwarted by the security measures in place at those facilities. Even in Damascus, where the embassy was an older facility that did not meet Inman standards, adequate security measures (aided by poor planning and execution on the part of the attackers) helped thwart a potentially disastrous attack.

However, in spite of the phrase "war on terrorism," terrorism is a tactic and not an entity. One cannot kill or destroy a tactic. Historically, terrorism has been used by a wide array of actors ranging from neo-Nazis to anarchists and from Maoists to jihadists. Even when the Cold War ended and many of the state-sponsored terrorist groups lost their funding, the tactic of terrorism endured. Even if the core al Qaeda leaders were killed or captured tomorrow and the jihadist threat were neutralized next week, terrorism would not go away. As we have previously pointed out, ideologies are far harder to kill than individuals. There will always be actors with various ideologies who will embrace terrorism as a tactic to strike a stronger enemy, and as the sole global superpower, the United States and its diplomatic missions will be targeted for terrorist attacks for the foreseeable future — or at least the next 100 years.

During this time, the booms and busts of counterterrorism and security spending will continue in response to successful attacks and in the lulls between spectacular terrorist strikes like 9/11. During the lulls in this cycle, it will be easy for complacency to slip in — especially when there are competing financial needs. But terrorism is not going to go away any time soon, and when emotion is removed from the cycle, a logical and compelling argument emerges for consistently supplying enough money to protect U.S. embassies and other essential facilities.

---

# AQAP: Paradigm Shifts and Lessons Learned
*Sept. 2, 2009*

On the evening of Aug. 28, Prince Mohammed bin Nayef, the Saudi Deputy Interior Minister — and the man in charge of the kingdom's counterterrorism efforts — was receiving members of the public in connection with the celebration of Ramadan, the Islamic month of fasting. As part of the Ramadan celebration, it is customary for members of the Saudi royal family to hold public gatherings where citizens can seek to settle disputes or offer Ramadan greetings.

One of the highlights of the Friday gathering was supposed to be the prince's meeting with Abdullah Hassan Taleh al-Asiri, a Saudi man who was a wanted militant from al Qaeda in the Arabian Peninsula (AQAP). Al-Asiri had allegedly renounced terrorism and had requested to meet the prince in order to repent and then be accepted into the kingdom's amnesty program. Such surrenders are not unprecedented — and they serve as great press events for the kingdom's ideological battle against jihadists. Prince Mohammed, who is responsible for the Saudi rehabilitation program for militants, is a key figure in that ideological battle.

In February, a man who appeared with al-Asiri on Saudi Arabia's list of most-wanted militants — former Guantanamo Bay inmate Mohammed al-Awfi — surrendered in Yemen and was transported to Saudi Arabia where he renounced terrorism and entered into the kingdom's amnesty program. Al-Awfi, who had appeared in a January 2009 video issued by the newly created AQAP after the merger of the Saudi and Yemeni nodes of the global jihadist network, was a senior AQAP leader, and his renouncement was a major blow against AQAP.

But the al-Asiri case ended very differently from the al-Awfi case. Unlike al-Awfi, al-Asiri was not a genuine repentant — he was a human Trojan horse. After al-Asiri entered a small room to speak with Prince Mohammed, he activated a small improvised explosive device (IED) he had been carrying inside his anal cavity. The resulting explosion ripped al-Asiri to shreds but only lightly injured the shocked prince — the target of al-Asiri's unsuccessful assassination attempt.

While the assassination proved unsuccessful, AQAP had been able to shift the operational paradigm in a manner that allowed them to achieve tactical surprise. The surprise was complete and the Saudis did not see the attack coming — the operation could have succeeded had it been better executed.

The kind of paradigm shift evident in this attack has far-reaching implications from a protective-intelligence standpoint, and security services will have to adapt in order to counter the new tactics employed. The attack also allows some important conclusions to be drawn about AQAP's ability to operate inside Saudi Arabia.

## Paradigm Shifts

Militants conducting terrorist attacks and the security services attempting to guard against such attacks have long engaged in a tactical game of cat and mouse. As militants adopt new tactics, security measures are then implemented to counter those tactics. The security changes then cause the militants to change in response and the cycle begins again. These changes can include using different weapons, employing weapons in a new way or changing the type of targets selected.

Sometimes, militants will implement a new tactic or series of tactics that is so revolutionary that it completely changes the framework of assumptions — or the paradigm — under which the security forces operate. Historically, al Qaeda and its jihadist progeny have proved to be very good at understanding the security paradigm and then developing tactics intended to exploit vulnerabilities in that paradigm in order to launch surprise attacks. For example:

- Prior to the 9/11 attacks, it was inconceivable that a large passenger aircraft would be used as a manually operated cruise missile. Hence, security screeners allowed box cutters to be carried onto aircraft, which were then used by the hijackers to take over the planes.

- The use of faux journalists to assassinate Ahmed Shah Masood with suicide IEDs hidden in their camera gear was also quite inventive.

- Had Richard Reid been able to light the fuse on his shoe bomb, we might still be wondering what happened to American Airlines Flight 63.

- The boat bomb employed against the USS Cole in October 2000 was another example of a paradigm shift that resulted in tactical surprise.

Once the element of tactical surprise is lost, however, the new tactics can be countered:

- When the crew and passengers on United Airlines Flight 93 learned what had happened to the other flights hijacked and flown to New York and Washington on Sept. 11, 2001, they stormed the cockpit and stopped the hijackers from using their aircraft in an attack. Aircraft cockpit doors have also been hardened and other procedural measures have been put in place to make 9/11-style suicide hijackings harder to pull off.

- Following the Masood assassination, journalists have been given very close scrutiny before being allowed into the proximity of a VIP.

- The traveling public has felt the impact of the Reid shoe-bombing attempt by being forced to remove their shoes every time they pass through airport security. And the thwarted 2006 Heathrow plot has resulted in limits on the size of liquid containers travelers can take aboard aircraft.

- The U.S. Navy is now very careful to guard against small craft pulling up alongside its warships.

Let's now take a look at the paradigm shift marked by the Prince Mohammed assassination attempt.

## AQAP's Tactical Innovations

First, using a repentant militant was a brilliant move, especially when combined with the timing of Ramadan. For Muslims, Ramadan is a time for introspection, sacrifice, reconciliation and repentance — it is a time to exercise self-restraint and practice good deeds. Additionally, as previously mentioned, Ramadan is a time when the Saudi royal family customarily makes itself more accessible to the people than at other times of the year. By using a repentant militant who appears on Saudi Arabia's list of most-wanted militants, AQAP was playing to the ego of the Saudis, who very much want to crush AQAP, and who also want to use AQAP members who have renounced terrorism and the group as part of their ideological campaign against jihadists. The surrender of an AQAP member offered the Saudi government a prize and a useful tool — it was an attractive offer and, as anticipated, Prince Mohammed took the bait. (Another side benefit of this tactic from the perspective of AQAP is that it will make the Saudis far more careful when they are dealing with surrendered militants in the future.)

The second tactical innovation in this case was the direct targeting of a senior member of the Saudi royal family and the member of the family specifically charged with leading the campaign against AQAP. In the past, jihadist militants in Saudi Arabia have targeted foreign interests and energy infrastructure in the kingdom. While jihadists have long derided and threatened the Saudi royal family in public statements, including AQAP statements released this year, they had not, prior to the Prince Mohammed assassination attempt, ever tried to follow through on any of their threats. Nor has the group staged any successful attack inside the kingdom since the February 2007 attack that killed four French citizens, and it has not attempted a major attack in Saudi Arabia since the failed February 2006 attack against a major oil-processing facility in the city of Abqaiq. Certainly the group had never before attempted a specifically targeted assassination against any member of the very large Saudi royal family — much less a senior member. Therefore the attack against Prince Mohammed came as a complete surprise. There are many less senior members of the royal family who would have been far more vulnerable to attack, but they would not have carried the rank or symbolism that Mohammed does.

But aside from his rank, Mohammed was the logical target to select for this operation because of his office and how he conducts his duties. Mohammed has long served as the primary contact between jihadists and the Saudi government, and he is the person Saudi militants go to in order to surrender. He has literally met with hundreds of repentant jihadists in person and had experienced no known security issues prior to the Aug. 28 incident. This explains why Mohammed personally spoke on the phone with al-Asiri prior to the surrender and why he did not express much concern over meeting with someone who appeared on his government's list of most-wanted militants. He met with such men regularly.

Since it is well known that Mohammed has made it his personal mission to handle surrendering militants, AQAP didn't have to do much intelligence work to realize that Mohammed was vulnerable to an attack or to arrange for a booby-trapped al-Asiri to meet with Mohammed. They merely had to adapt their tactics in order to exploit vulnerabilities in the security paradigm.

The third tactical shift is perhaps the most interesting, and that is the use of an IED hidden in the anal cavity of the bomber. Suicide bombers have long been creative when it comes to hiding their devices. In addition to the above-mentioned IED in the camera gear used in the Masood assassination, female suicide bombers with the Liberation Tigers of Tamil Eelam have hidden IEDs inside brassieres, and female suicide bombers with the Kurdistan Workers' Party have worn IEDs designed to make them look pregnant. However, this is the first instance we are aware of where a suicide bomber has hidden an IED inside a body cavity.

It is fairly common practice around the world for people to smuggle contraband such as drugs inside their body cavities. This is done not only to get items across international borders but also to get contraband into prisons. It is not unusual for people to smuggle narcotics and even cell phones into prisons inside their body cavities (the prison slang for this practice is "keistering"). It is also not at all uncommon for inmates to keister weapons such as knives or improvised stabbing devices known as "shanks." Such keistered items can be very difficult to detect using standard search methods, especially if they do not contain much metal.

In the case of al-Asiri, he turned himself in to authorities on the afternoon of Aug. 27 and did not meet with Mohammed until the evening of Aug. 28. By the time al-Asiri detonated his explosive device, he had been in custody for some 30 hours and had been subjected to several security searches, though it is unlikely that any of them included a body cavity search. While it is possible that there was some type of internal collusion, it is more likely that the device had been hidden inside of al-Asiri the entire time.

AQAP's claim of responsibility for the attack included the following statement: "…Abdullah Hassan Taleh al-Asiri, who was on the list of 85 wanted persons, was able, with the help of God, to enter Nayef's palace as he was among his guards and detonate an explosive device. No one will be able to know the type of this device or the way it was detonated. Al-Asiri managed to pass all the security checkpoints in Najran and Jeddah airports and was transported on board Mohammed bin Nayef's private plane."

AQAP also threatened additional surprise attacks in the "near future," but now that the type of device al-Asiri used is known, security measures can — and almost certainly will — be implemented to prevent similar attacks in the future.

While keistering an IED is a novel tactic, it does present operational planners with some limitations. For one thing, the amount of explosive material that can be hidden inside a person is far less than the amount that can be placed inside a backpack or is typically used in a suicide belt or vest. For another, the body of the bomber will tend to absorb much of the blast wave and most of any fragmentation from the device. This means that the bomber would have to get in very close proximity to an intended target in order to kill him or her. Such a device would not be very useful for a mass-casualty attack like the July 17 Jakarta hotel bombings and instead would be more useful in assassination attempts against targeted individuals.

We have not been able to determine exactly how the device was triggered, but it likely employed a command-detonated remote device of some kind. Having wires protruding from the bomber's body would be a sure giveaway. The use of a wireless remote means that the device would be susceptible to radio frequency countermeasures.

One other concern about such a device is that it would likely have a catastrophic result if employed on an aircraft, especially if it were removed from the bomber's body and placed in a strategic location on board the aircraft. Richard Reid's shoe IED only contained about four ounces of explosives, an amount that could conceivably be smuggled inside a human.

## What the Attack Says About AQAP

While the Aug. 28 attack highlighted AQAP's operational creativity, it also demonstrated that the group failed to effectively execute the attack after gaining the element of surprise. Quite simply, the bomber detonated his device too far away from the intended target. It is quite likely that the group failed to do adequate testing with the device and did not know what its effective kill radius was. AQAP will almost certainly attempt to remedy that error before it tries to employ such a device again.

In the larger picture, this attempt shows that AQAP does not have the resources inside the kingdom to plan and execute an attack on a figure like Prince Mohammed. That it would try a nuanced and highly targeted strike against Mohammed rather than a more brazen armed assault or vehicle-borne IED attack demonstrates that the group is very weak inside Saudi Arabia. It even needed to rely on operatives and planners who were in Yemen to execute the attack.

When the formation of AQAP was announced in January, STRATFOR noted that it would be important to watch for indications of whether the merger of the Saudi and Yemeni groups was a sign of desperation by a declining group or an indication that it had new blood and was on the rise. AQAP's assassination attempt on Prince Mohammed has clearly demonstrated that the group is weak and in decline.

AQAP has not given up the struggle, but the group will be hard-pressed to weather the storm that is about to befall it as the Saudis retaliate for the plot. It will be very surprising if it is able to carry through with its threat to attack other members of the Saudi royal family in the near future. Indeed, the very fact that AQAP has threatened more attacks on the royal family likely indicates that the threats are empty; if the group truly did have other plots in the works, it would not want to risk jeopardizing those plots by prompting the Saudis to increase security in response to a threat.

Lacking the strength to conduct large, aggressive attacks, the weakened AQAP will need to continue innovating in order to pose a threat to the Saudi monarchy. But, as seen in the Aug. 28 case, tactical innovation requires more than just a novel idea — militants must also carefully develop and test new concepts before they can use them to effectively conduct a terrorist attack.

---

# Counterterrorism: Shifting from the 'Who' to the 'How'
### *Nov. 4, 2009*

In the 11th edition of the online magazine Sada al-Malahim (The Echo of Battle), which was released to jihadist Web sites last week, al Qaeda in the Arabian Peninsula (AQAP) leader Nasir al-Wahayshi wrote an article that called for jihadists to conduct simple attacks against a variety of targets. The targets included "any tyrant, intelligence den, prince" or "minister" (referring to the governments in the Muslim world like Egypt, Saudi Arabia and Yemen), and "any crusaders whenever you find one of them, like at the airports of the crusader Western countries that participate in the wars against Islam, or their living compounds, trains etc." (an obvious reference to the United States and Europe and Westerners living in Muslim countries).

Al-Wahayshi, an ethnic Yemeni who spent time in Afghanistan serving as a lieutenant under Osama bin Laden, noted these simple attacks could be conducted with readily available weapons such as knives, clubs or small improvised explosive devices (IEDs). According to al-Wahayshi, jihadists "don't need to conduct a big effort or spend a lot of money to manufacture 10 grams of explosive material" and they should not "waste a long time finding the materials, because you can find all these in your mother's kitchen, or readily at hand or in any city you are in."

That al-Wahayshi gave these instructions in an Internet magazine distributed via jihadist chat rooms, not in some secret meeting with his operational staff, demonstrates that they are clearly intended to reach grassroots jihadists — and are not intended as some sort of internal guidance for AQAP members. In fact, al-Wahayshi was encouraging grassroots jihadists to "do what Abu al-Khair did," referring to AQAP member Abdullah Hassan Taleh al-Asiri, the Saudi suicide bomber who attempted to kill Saudi Deputy Interior Minister Prince Mohammed bin Nayef with a small IED on Aug. 28.

The most troubling aspect of al-Wahayshi's statement is that it is largely true. Improvised explosive mixtures are, in fact, relatively easy to make from readily available chemicals — if a person has the proper training — and attacks using small IEDs or other readily attainable weapons such as knives or clubs (or firearms in the United States) are indeed quite simple to conduct.

As STRATFOR has noted for several years now, with al Qaeda's structure under continual attack and no regional al Qaeda franchise groups in the Western Hemisphere, the most pressing jihadist threat to the U.S. homeland at present stems from grassroots jihadists, not the al Qaeda core. This trend has been borne out by the large number of plots and arrests over the past several years, including several so far in 2009. The grassroots have likewise proved to pose a critical threat to Europe (although it is important to note that, while the threat posed by grassroots operatives is more widespread, it normally involves smaller, less strategic attacks than those conducted by the al Qaeda core).

From a counterterrorism perspective, the problem posed by grassroots operatives is that, unless they somehow self-identify by contacting a government informant or another person who reports them to authorities, attend a militant training camp, or conduct electronic correspondence with a person or organization under government scrutiny, they are very difficult to detect.

The threat posed by grassroots operatives, and the difficulty identifying them, highlight the need for counterterrorism programs to adopt a proactive, protective intelligence approach to the problem — an approach that focuses on the "how" of militant attacks instead of just the "who."

## The How

In the traditional, reactive approach to counterterrorism, where authorities respond to a crime scene after a terrorist attack to find and arrest the militants responsible for the attack, it is customary to focus on the who, or on the individual or group behind the attack. Indeed, in this approach, the only time much emphasis is placed on the how is either in an effort to identify a suspect when an unknown actor carried out the attack or to prove, during a trial, that a particular suspect was responsible for the attack. Beyond these limited purposes, not much attention is paid to the how.

In large part, this focus on the who is a legacy of the fact that for many years, the primary philosophy of the U.S. government was to treat counterterrorism as a law-enforcement program, with a focus on prosecution rather than on disrupting plots.

Certainly, catching and prosecuting those who commit terrorist attacks is necessary, but from our perspective, preventing attacks is more important, and prevention requires a proactive approach. To pursue such a proactive approach to counterterrorism, the how becomes a critical question. By studying and understanding how attacks are conducted — i.e., the exact steps and actions required for a successful attack — authorities can establish systems to proactively identify early indicators that planning for an attack is under way. People involved in planning the attack can then be focused on and identified, and action can be taken to prevent them from conducting the attack. This means that focusing on the how can lead to previously unidentified suspects, e.g., those who do not self-identify.

"How was the attack conducted?" is the primary question addressed by protective intelligence, which is, at its core, a process for proactively identifying and assessing potential threats. Focusing on the how, then, requires protective intelligence practitioners to carefully study the tactics, tradecraft and behavior associated with militant actors involved in terrorist attacks. This allows them to search for and identify those behaviors before an attack takes place. Many of these behaviors are not by themselves criminal in nature; visiting a public building and observing security measures or standing on the street to watch the arrival of a VIP at his or her office are not illegal acts, but they can be indicators that an attack is being plotted. Such legal activities ultimately could be overt actions in furtherance of an illegal conspiracy to conduct the attack, but even where conspiracy cannot be proved, steps can still be taken to identify possible assailants and prevent a potential attack — or, at the very least, to mitigate the risk posed by the people involved.

Protective intelligence is based on the fact that successful attacks don't just happen out of the blue. Rather, terrorist attacks follow a discernible attack cycle. There are critical points during that cycle where a plot is most likely to be detected by an outside observer. Some of the points during the attack cycle when potential attackers are most vulnerable to detection are while surveillance is being conducted and weapons are being acquired. However, there are other, less obvious points where people on the lookout can spot preparations for an attack.

It is true that sometimes individuals do conduct ill-conceived, poorly executed attacks that involve shortcuts in the planning process. But this type of spur-of-the-moment attack is usually associated with mentally disturbed individuals, and it is extremely rare for a militant actor to conduct a spontaneous terrorist attack without first following the steps of the attack cycle.

To really understand the how, protective intelligence practitioners cannot simply acknowledge that something like surveillance occurs. Rather, they must turn a powerful lens on steps like pre-operational surveillance to gain an in-depth understanding of those steps. Dissecting an activity like pre-operational surveillance requires not only examining subjects such as the demeanor demonstrated by those conducting surveillance prior to an attack and the specific methods and cover for action and status used. It also requires identifying particular times where surveillance is most likely and certain optimal vantage points (called "perches" in surveillance jargon) from where a surveillant is most likely to operate when trying to surveil a specific facility or event. This type of complex understanding of surveillance can then be used to help focus human or technological countersurveillance efforts where they can be most effective.

Unfortunately, many counterterrorism investigators are so focused on the who that they do not focus on collecting this type of granular how information. When we have spoken with law enforcement officers responsible for investigating recent grassroots plots, they have given us blank stares in response to questions about how the suspects had conducted surveillance on the intended targets. They simply had not paid attention to this type of detail — but this oversight is not really the investigators' fault. No one had ever explained to them why paying attention to, and recording, this type of detail was important. Moreover, it takes specific training and a practiced eye to observe and record these details without glossing over them. For example, it is quite useful if a protective intelligence officer has first conducted a lot of surveillance, because conducting surveillance allows one to understand what a surveillant must do and where he must be in order to effectively observe surveillance of a specific person or place.

Similarly, to truly understand the tradecraft required to build an IED and the specific steps a militant must take to do so, it helps to go to an IED school where the investigator learns the tradecraft firsthand. Militant actors can and do change over time. New groups, causes and ideologies emerge, and specific militants can be killed, captured or retire. But the tactical steps a militant must complete to conduct a successful attack are constant. It doesn't matter if the person planning an attack is a radical environmentalist, a grassroots jihadist or a member of the al Qaeda core. While these diverse actors will exhibit different levels of professionalism regarding terrorist tradecraft, they still must follow essentially the same steps, accomplish the same tasks and operate in the same areas. Knowing this allows protective intelligence to guard against different levels of threats.

Of course, tactics can be changed and perfected and new tactics can be developed (often in response to changes in security and law enforcement operations). Additionally, new technologies can emerge (like cell phones and Google Earth) that can alter the way some of these activities are conducted, or reduce the time it takes to complete them. Studying the tradecraft and behaviors needed to execute evolving tactics, however, allows protective intelligence practitioners to respond to such changes and even alter how they operate in order to more effectively search for potential hostile activity.

Technology aids not only those trying to conduct attacks. There are a variety of new tools, such as Trapwire, a software system designed to work with camera systems to help detect patterns of pre-operational surveillance, that can be focused on critical areas to help cut through the fog of noise and activity and draw attention to potential threats. These technological tools can help turn the tables on unknown plotters because they are designed to focus on the how. They will likely never replace human observation and experience, but they can serve as valuable aids to human perception.

Of course, protective intelligence does not have to be the sole responsibility of federal authorities specifically charged with counterterrorism. Corporate security managers and private security contractors should also apply these principles to protecting the people and facilities in their charge, as should local and state police agencies. In a world full of soft targets — and given the limited resources available to protect those targets — the more eyes looking for such activity the better. Even the general public has an important role to play in practicing situational awareness and spotting potential terrorist activity.

## Keeping It Simple?

Al-Wahayshi is right that it is not difficult to construct improvised explosives from a wide range of household chemicals like peroxide and acetone or chlorine and brake fluid. He is also correct that some of those explosive mixtures can be concealed in objects ranging from electronic items to picture frames, or can be employed in many forms, from hand grenades to suicide vests. Likewise, low-level attacks can also be conducted using knives, clubs and guns.

Furthermore, when grassroots jihadists plan and carry out attacks acting as lone wolves or in small compartmentalized cells without inadvertently betraying their mission by conspiring with people known to the authorities, they are not able to be detected by the who-focused systems, and it becomes far more difficult to discover and thwart these plots. This focus on the how absolutely does not mean that who-centered programs must be abandoned. Surveillance on known militants, their associates and their communications should continue, efforts to identify people attending militant training camps or fighting in places like Afghanistan or Somalia must be increased, and people who conduct terrorist attacks should be identified and prosecuted.

However — and this is an important however — if an unknown militant is going to conduct even a simple attack against some of the targets al-Wahayshi suggests, such as an airport, train or specific leader or media personality, complexity creeps into the picture, and the planning cycle must be followed if an attack is going to be successful. The prospective attacker must observe and quantify the target, construct a plan for the attack and then execute that plan. The demands of this process will force even an attacker previously unknown to the authorities into a position where he is vulnerable to discovery. If the attacker does this while there are people watching for such activity, he will likely be seen. But if he does this while no one is watching, there is little chance that he will become a who until after the attack has been completed.

# Profiling: Sketching the Face of Jihadism
*Jan. 20, 2010*

On Jan. 4, 2010, the U.S. Transportation Security Administration (TSA) adopted new rules that would increase the screening of citizens from 14 countries who want to fly to the United States as well as travelers of all nationalities who are flying to the United States from one of the 14 countries. These countries are: Afghanistan, Algeria, Cuba, Iran, Iraq, Lebanon, Libya, Nigeria, Pakistan, Saudi Arabia, Somalia, Sudan, Syria and Yemen.

Four of the countries — Cuba, Iran, Sudan and Syria — are on the U.S. government's list of state sponsors of terrorism. The other 10 have been labeled "countries of interest" by the TSA and appear to have been added in response to jihadist attacks in recent years. Nigeria was almost certainly added to the list only as a result of the Christmas Day bombing attempt aboard a Detroit-bound U.S. airliner by Umar Farouk Abdulmutallab, a 23-year-old Nigerian man.

As reflected by the large number of chain e-mails that swirl around after every attack or attempted attack against the United States, the type of profiling program the TSA has instituted will be very popular in certain quarters. Conventional wisdom holds that such programs will be effective in protecting the flying public from terrorist attacks because profiling is easy to do. However, when one steps back and carefully examines the historical face of the jihadist threat, it becomes readily apparent that it is very difficult to create a one-size-fits-all profile of a jihadist operative. When focusing on a resourceful and adaptive adversary, the use of such profiles sets a security system up for failure by causing security personnel and the general public to focus on a threat that is defined too narrowly.

Sketching the face of jihadism is simply not as easy as it might seem.

## The Historical Face of Terror

One popular chain e-mail that seemingly circulates after every attack or attempted attack notes that the attack was not made or attempted by Richard Simmons or the Tooth Fairy but by "Muslim male extremists between the ages of 17 and 40." And when we set aside the Chechen "Black Widows," the occasional female suicide bomber and people like Timothy McVeigh and Eric Rudolph, many terrorist attacks are indeed planned and orchestrated by male Muslim extremists between the ages of 17 and 40. The problem comes when you try to define what a male Muslim extremist between the ages of 17 and 40 looks like.

When we look back at the early jihadist attacks against the United States, we see that many perpetrators matched the stereotypical Muslim profile. In the killing of Rabbi Meir Kahane, the 1993 World Trade Center bombing and the thwarted 1993 New York Landmarks Plot, we saw a large contingent of Egyptians, including Omar Abdul-Rahman (aka "the Blind Sheikh"), El Sayyid Nosair, Ibrahim Elgabrowny, Mahmud Abouhalima and several others. In fact, Egyptians played a significant role in the development of the jihadist ideology and have long constituted a very substantial portion of the international jihadist movement — and even of the core al Qaeda cadre. Because of this, it is quite surprising that Egypt does not appear on the TSA's profile list.

Indeed, in addition to the Egyptians, in the early jihadist plots against the United States we also saw operatives who were Palestinian, Pakistani, Sudanese and Iraqi. However — and this is significant — in the New York Landmarks Plot we also saw a Puerto Rican convert to Islam named Victor Alvarez and an African-American Muslim named Clement Rodney Hampton-el. Alvarez and Hampton-el clearly did not fit the typical profile.

The Kuwait-born Pakistani citizen who was the bombmaker in the 1993 World Trade Center bombing is a man named Abdul Basit (widely known by his alias, Ramzi Yousef). After leaving the United States, Basit resettled in Manila and attempted to orchestrate an attack against U.S. airliners in Asia called Operation Bojinka. After an apartment fire in Manila caused Basit to flee the city, he moved to Islamabad, where he attempted to recruit new jihadist operatives to carry out the Bojinka plot. One of the men he recruited was a South African Muslim named Istaique Parker. After a few dry-run operations, Parker got cold feet, decided he did not want to embrace martyrdom and helped the U.S. Diplomatic Security Service special agents assigned to the U.S. Embassy orchestrate Basit's arrest. A South African named Parker does not fit the typical terrorist profile.

The following individuals, among many others, were involved in jihadist activity but did not fit what most people would consider the typical jihadist profile:

- Richard Reid, the British citizen known as the "shoe bomber."
- Jose Padilla, the American citizen known as the "dirty bomber."
- Adam Gadahn, an al Qaeda spokesman who was born Adam Pearlman in California.
- John Walker Lindh, the so-called "American Taliban."
- Jack Roche, the Australian known as "Jihad Jack."
- The Duka brothers, ethnic Albanians involved in the Fort Dix plot.
- Daniel Boyd and his sons, American citizens plotting grass-roots attacks inside the United States.
- Germaine Maurice Lindsay, the Jamaican-born suicide bomber involved in the July 7, 2005, London attacks.
- Nick Reilly, the British citizen who attempted to bomb a restaurant in Exeter in May 2008.
- David Headley, the U.S. citizen who helped plan the Mumbai attacks.

As reflected by the list above, jihadists come from many ethnicities and nationalities, and they can range from Americans named

Daniel, Victor or John to a Macedonian nicknamed "Elvis," a Tanzanian called "Foopie" (who smuggled explosives by bicycle) and an Indonesian named Zulkarnaen. There simply is not one ethnic or national profile that can be used to describe them all.

## An Adaptive Opponent

One of the big reasons we've witnessed men with names like Richard and Jose used in jihadist plots is because jihadist planners are adaptive and innovative. They will adjust the operatives they select for a mission in order to circumvent new security measures. In the wake of the 9/11 attacks, when security forces began to focus additional scrutiny on people with Muslim names, they dispatched Richard Reid on his shoe-bomb mission. And it worked — Reid was able to get his device by security and onto the plane. If he hadn't fumbled the execution of the attack, it would have destroyed the aircraft. Moreover, when Khalid Sheikh Mohammed wanted to get an operative into the United States to conduct attacks following 9/11, he selected U.S. citizen Jose Padilla. Padilla successfully entered the country, and it was only Mohammed's arrest and interrogation that alerted authorities to Padilla's mission.

But their operational flexibility in fact predates the 9/11 attack. For example, some of the operatives initially selected for the 9/11 mission were Yemenis and could not obtain visas to the United States. Since Saudis were able to obtain visas much easier, al Qaeda simply shifted gears and decided to use Saudis instead of Yemenis.

Pakistan-based militant groups Lashkar-e-Taiba and Harkat-ul-Jihad e-Islami likewise sought to fool the Danish and Indian security services when they dispatched an American citizen named David Headley from Chicago to conduct pre-operational surveillance in Mumbai and Denmark. Headley, who was named Daood Gilani at his birth, legally changed his name to David Coleman Headley, anglicizing his first name and taking his mother's maiden name. The name change and his American accent were apparently enough to throw intelligence agencies off his trail — in spite of his very aggressive surveillance activity.

Most recently, al Qaeda in the Arabian Peninsula (AQAP) showed its cunning when it dispatched a Nigerian, Abdulmutallab, in the Christmas Day attack. Although STRATFOR was among the first to see the threat AQAP's innovative devices posed to aviation security, there is no way we could have forecast that the group would conduct an attack originating out of Nigeria using a Nigerian citizen. A Saudi or Yemeni, certainly; a Somali or American citizen, maybe — but a Nigerian? AQAP's use of such an operative was a total paradigm shift. (Perhaps this paradigm shift explains in part why U.S. officials chose not to act more aggressively on intelligence they had obtained on Abdulmutallab that could have prevented the attack.) The only reason Nigeria is on the list of 14 countries now is because of the Christmas Day incident, and there is no reason that jihadists couldn't use a Muslim from Togo, Ghana, or Trinidad and Tobago instead of a Nigerian in their next attack.

Jihadist planners have now heard about the list of 14 countries and, demonstrating their adaptability, will undoubtedly try to use operatives who are not from one of those countries and choose flights that originate from other places as well. They may even follow the lead of Chechen militants and the Islamic State of Iraq by employing female suicide bombers. They will also likely instruct operatives to "lose" their passports so that they can obtain new documents that contain no traces of travel to one of the 14 countries on the list. Jihadists have frequently used this tactic to hide operatives' travel to training camps in places like Afghanistan and Pakistan.

Moreover, jihadist groups have no lack of operatives from countries that are not on that list. Jihadists from all over the world have traveled to jihadist training camps, and in addition to the large number of Egyptian, Moroccan and Tunisian jihadists (countries not on the list), there are also Filipinos, Indonesians, Malaysians and, of course, Americans and Europeans. Frankly, there have been far more jihadist plots that have originated in the United Kingdom than there have been plots involving Nigerians, and yet Nigeria is on the list and the United Kingdom is not. Because of this, a British citizen (or an American, for that matter) who has been fighting with al Shabaab in Somalia could board a flight in Nairobi or Cairo and receive less scrutiny than an innocent Nigerian flying from the same airport.

In an environment where the potential threat is hard to identify, it is doubly important to profile individuals based on their behavior rather than their ethnicity or nationality — what we refer to as focusing on the "how" rather than the "who." Instead of relying on pat profiles, security personnel should be encouraged to exercise their intelligence, intuition and common sense. A U.S. citizen named Robert who shows up at the U.S. Embassy in Nairobi or Amman claiming to have lost his passport may be far more dangerous than some random Pakistani or Yemeni citizen, even though the American does not fit the profile requiring extra security checks.

The difficulty of creating a reliable and accurate physical profile of a jihadist, and the adaptability and ingenuity of the jihadist planners, means that any attempt at profiling is doomed to fail. In fact, profiling can prove counterproductive to good security by blinding people to real threats. They will dismiss potential malefactors who do not fit the specific profile they have been provided.

# CHAPTER 2: THE ART OF SURVEILLANCE

---

## Surveillance: For Good — and Evil
### *Dec. 17, 2005*

Whether terrorists are attempting to assassinate a high-ranking government official, bring down a building or explode a bomb in a subway, their first order of business is to determine how best to set up the attack. To make such a determination, pre-operational surveillance of the target is vital.

If the target is a person, surveillance will determine his or her patterns of behavior; for a building, subway or other facility, the surveillance would help define possible weaknesses. In this way, attackers can determine the best time, location and method for the attack, how best to take advantage of the element of surprise — and how to escape afterward.

Terrorists, of course, are not alone in this regard. Carrying out an attack of any kind — a bank robbery, purse snatching or kidnapping, for example — requires that the perpetrators eye their target in advance, although the extent of the surveillance and its complexity will vary depending on the scale of the operation and the end goal. A purse snatcher, for example, might size up the victim for only a few seconds, while terrorists could assign a special team for this specific mission and then take up to several weeks to get the job done.

Kidnappers and assassins also conduct surveillance of varying lengths to understand the target's daily routine, including the time he leaves the house in the morning and the route he takes to work.

U.S. and Jordanian intelligence indicates that the cell involved in the Nov. 9 suicide bombings in Amman, Jordan, conducted surveillance on all three hotels involved, though details about the length and degree of surveillance remain murky. The perpetrators of the April 1992 kidnapping of Exxon executive Sidney Reso conducted extensive surveillance and found that Reso was most vulnerable when he reached the end of his driveway on the way to work in the morning. Reso died while in captivity.

Stalkers or mentally disturbed individuals who fixate on someone surveil their victims in advance, although in many cases the stalker wants to get caught and thus does not need to be looking for possible escape routes. Also, a stalker usually strikes impulsively with little consideration given to the consequences. Stalkers or lone wolf attackers generally will conduct surveillance alone, making them difficult, but not impossible, to spot.

A great deal of surveillance also is conducted for purposes of collecting information. U.S. government employees and American businesspeople and business facilities overseas are routinely subjected to surveillance by local intelligence agencies in places such as China, France and Israel. The goal here is economic espionage aimed at keeping abreast of business activities — and stealing business secrets. Industrial spies, though working for themselves or for private concerns, have similar goals. Private investigators routinely observe people and places for their clients, usually to link an individual to a particular activity or event.

Not all surveillance is conducted for nefarious purposes, however. On the contrary, surveillance is an integral part of U.S. law enforcement and intelligence operations designed to prevent criminal and terrorist activity. Security personnel place closed-circuit TV in retail stores and banks to deter criminals, while police officers stake out certain street corners to keep tabs on drug-traffickers, for instance.

Surveillance is a fact of life in the 21st century. In many ways, technological advances have made it easier for law enforcement to protect citizens. These advances, however, also have made it easier for those who wish to do harm.

---

# The Spread of Technical Surveillance
## *Dec. 21, 2005*

As far back as the 5th century B.C., Chinese warrior-philosopher Sun Tzu went on record citing the paramount importance of using spies and clandestine reconnaissance to uncover enemy plans. At the time — and for centuries afterward — surveillance involved placing an operative close enough to a target to track his movements or overhear his conversations. Technological advances — especially those that have come along over the past century — have made it possible not only to watch and listen to others from afar but also to do so with ease.

Today, technical surveillance is conducted for a wide variety of purposes by individuals as diverse as terrorists, private investigators, activists, paparazzi, peeping toms, law enforcement personnel and governments agents — and even by parents who listen in on their infants via baby monitors. These people are tracking a subject's activities, usually from a distance or remotely, using devices specifically designed or adapted for that purpose such as global positioning system (GPS) locators, sophisticated listening devices and cameras of all kinds.

Al Qaeda used technical surveillance when targeting financial institutions in Washington, D.C., New York and Newark, N.J., and potential targets in Singapore in 2003. In New York, for example, several operatives sat in a Starbucks café across the street from their intended target and recorded various aspects of the institution's security measures and building access. Their notes and some of their videos were found on a laptop computer after authorities broke up the cell. Although al Qaeda uses less-sophisticated technology than some — hand-held cameras versus micro-cameras and bionic ears, for example — the network's ability to conduct technical surveillance still is formidable.

Environmental activists, animal rights activists, anarchists and anti-globalization activists frequently surveil their subjects before staging a protest or "direct action" operations. Groups that target corporations for sabotage, such as the Earth Liberation Front, are especially sophisticated in the use of technical surveillance.

The Ruckus Society is a group devoted to training activists in "electronic scouting" — technical surveillance involving the use of remote cameras, GPS locators, frequency counters, programmable scanners and night-vision goggles. Program graduates utilize high-tech equipment such as miniature remote cameras and "bionic ear" listening devices to conduct their surveillance. These activists frequently use programmable scanners and cameras to monitor security/police communications and activity in order to warn the saboteurs of an impeding response by law enforcement.

In some countries, it is not uncommon for Western business or government travelers to find telltale signs of listening devices in their hotel rooms, offices, meeting rooms and chauffeur-driven cars. In other instances, people have been caught spying on others in public bathrooms and changing rooms using tiny cameras that can be concealed in something as seemingly innocuous as an air freshener or electrical outlet.

The accessibility and miniature size of today's surveillance equipment makes it easy for just about anyone to clandestinely watch someone else. As technology continues to advance and surveillance becomes even more ubiquitous, methods to thwart such eavesdropping also will improve.

# Physical Surveillance: Tailing Someone on the Move
*Dec. 22, 2005*

The image of the darkly clad private eye slipping in and out of doorways as he surreptitiously tails his subject around the busy city is straight out of the movies. The fact is, however, that physical surveillance often is carried out this way — using a lot of shoe leather. Technological advances and expert training in stealth have made the job easier than in the past, but when it comes down to it, there is no other way to keep an eye on a subject who is on the move.

Technical surveillance is carried out remotely, usually through video or audio recording equipment, when the subject remains in one place, such as a hotel room, home or office. Physical surveillance, on the other hand, is performed by human operatives, and often involves observing the subject's actions as he travels around outside the home or office.

In fact, private investigators lack the enormous human and technical resources needed to get the job done right. This type of surveillance requires a large number of highly trained operatives who must be constantly trained as improvements in techniques are implemented. And this requires a significant support structure of instructors, facilities, money and material, as well as a well-developed network of communications to link the operatives together.

Physical surveillance can be broken down into two categories: static and mobile. Static surveillance favors the home team and puts a visitor or newcomer to the scene of the surveillance at a disadvantage. If the operatives conducting the surveillance are familiar with the area, they can better blend in with the local scenery, and thus be harder to detect. They also can better anticipate their subject's moves. The Soviets used static surveillance against U.S. Embassy personnel in Moscow during the Cold War. On the other hand, if the subject is local and the operatives are from outside the area, the advantage goes to the subject, who would be in a better position to spot people in his environment who do not fit in — especially in small settings.

However, static surveillance — when carried out properly — is difficult to detect because good surveillance operatives blend in with their surroundings and make themselves as innocuous as possible. As creatures of habit, most people get used to their surroundings and fail to notice things they see every day. By blending in with the scenery the subject sees every day, such as the local neighborhood or route taken every morning to work, the operative can effectively become invisible. Because of this, static surveillance requires a high degree of situational awareness — and a certain amount of paranoia — to detect.

Although static surveillance is the hardest type to detect and counter, it is expensive, since it can involve renting apartments, stores, street vendor kiosks and carts and other similar observation posts, known as "perches" in surveillance jargon. Because the operatives do not move, static surveillance requires that operatives be perched at close intervals so they can keep a constant eye on the target. In general, only governments have the manpower and resources necessary to do this type of surveillance properly.

Mobile surveillance can be carried out in two ways: in vehicles or on foot. A wider area can be covered in vehicular surveillance — and is vital if the subject is traveling by car — although this type of surveillance does have limitations. Should the subject go into an office building, a subway or a shopping mall, for example, the operatives in the vehicle cannot follow. Because of this limitation, vehicular surveillance is usually carried out in conjunction with foot surveillance. The operatives on foot are in communication with the operatives in the vehicle. In addition, the operatives in the vehicle will often drop off one of their team members to continue following the target. Mixed car/foot operations are effective because the target more often will focus on other pedestrians rather than the cars around him.

Depending on the resources available or allocated for a specific operation, mobile surveillance can range from an operative following the subject on foot — the hardest type of surveillance to accomplish without being detected — to an elaborate operation that puts the subject in a "bubble." The highest level involves multiple mobile and static surveillance teams all linked by communications and coordinating with one another to ensure that the subject's every movement is monitored — and that the team is not detected.

The bubble also provides protection against any erratic move the target might make to determine if he is being watched, or to ditch the surveillance. Therefore, if the team senses that the target has begun to "stair-step" (a series of deliberate turns intended to expose a surveillance team) through a residential neighborhood with very little activity on the street, the team using the bubble can wait outside the area instead of following the target through the maneuvers. Teams using a bubble will also frequently change "the eye" (the person directly watching the target) so that the target does not see the same face or vehicle twice. Again, in almost all cases, only a government has the resources and training to effectively provide this highest level of surveillance coverage.

In order to conduct surveillance uninterrupted over a long period of time, a combination of static and vehicular surveillance is often employed. Static surveillance operatives will stake out the subject's location — perhaps renting an apartment across the street from the person's home, and then give a "call out" to the mobile surveillance team when the subject moves. The static operative will advise the mobile team what direction the subject is going and if the subject is on foot or in a vehicle.

Physical surveillance — especially on a surveillance-aware target — is extremely difficult to carry out effectively, since it requires a great deal of training and practical experience. Criminals and terrorists who attempt to pull off an effective tail often lack the street skills to be effective, and often make mistakes that tip off the target. Because their objective can be to ambush — in order to kill or kidnap the subject — spotting physical surveillance is of critical importance.

# Physical Surveillance: The Art of Blending In
## Dec. 23, 2005

Role playing is an important aspect of undercover surveillance work — and those who attempt it without sufficient training often make mistakes that can alert their subject to the fact that they are being watched, or raise the suspicions of law enforcement or counter-surveillance teams.

Among the most common mistakes made by amateurs when conducting physical surveillance is the failure to get into proper character for the job or, when in character, to appear in places or carry out activities that are incongruent with the "costume." The terms used to describe these role-playing aspects of surveillance are "cover for status" and "cover for action." Good cover for status is an operative playing the role of a student studying in a coffee shop; bad cover for status is an operative dressed in business clothes walking in the woods. Good cover for action is an operative dressed as a telephone repairman pretending to work on phone lines — not playing chess in the park.

The purpose of using good cover for action and cover for status is to make the operative's presence look routine and normal. When done right, the operative fits in with the mental snapshot subconsciously taken by the subject as he goes about his business. Inexperienced surveillance operatives, or those without adequate resources, can be easily detected and their cover blown.

An acronym used by government agencies when training operatives in effective surveillance is TEDD: time, environment, distance and demeanor. Failure to take into account these four elements is another amateurish mistake that can get the operative caught. The factors of time, environment and distance are important because a subject who notices the same person hovering around again and again at different times and locations is more likely to become aware that he is being watched. Demeanor refers to lack of cover or simply bad body language — which also can alert a subject to the presence of a surveillance team.

A surveillance operative also must be extensively trained to avoid the so-called "burn syndrome," the erroneous belief that the subject has spotted him. Feeling burned will cause the operative to do unnatural things, such as suddenly ducking back into a doorway or turning around abruptly when he unexpectedly comes face to face with his target. People inexperienced in the art of surveillance find it difficult to control this natural reaction.

These are just a few of the many mistakes that amateurs can make while conducting physical surveillance. They also can tip off the subject as to their presence by simply lurking around an area with no reason to be there, by entering or leaving a building immediately after the subject, or simply by running in street clothes.

Surveillance operatives following the subject in a vehicle also can make many mistakes, including:

- Parking in the same spot for an extended period of time while sitting in the front seat.
- Starting and stopping as the target moves.
- Driving too slowly or too fast and making erratic moves or abrupt stops.
- Signaling a turn but not making it.
- Following a target through a red light.
- Using two-way radios, binoculars or cameras from a vehicle.
- Flashing headlights between vehicles.
- Maintaining the same distance from the target even at varying speeds.
- Pausing in traffic circles until the target vehicle has taken an exit.
- Vehicles closing on the target in heavy traffic but falling back in light traffic.

- Jumping from the vehicle when the subject stops his vehicle and gets out.
- Parking a vehicle but remaining in the car.
- Tipping off the subject as to a shift change by having one vehicle pull up and park while the other pulls away — especially in an area the subject knows well, such as near the home or office.

In general, because of the resources and extensive training required to avoid making these mistakes, only governments have the time and resources to make surveillance operations highly effective. Even then, some very basic mistakes can be made that can alert the subject to the presence of a surveillance operation.

---

## Turning the Tables on Surveillants
### Dec. 31, 2005

Victims of planned hostile actions — such as kidnappings or killings — almost always are closely monitored by their attackers in advance of the operation. Such pre-operational surveillance enables the plotters to determine the best method of attack, as well as the best time and place to carry it out. Savvy countersurveillance, however, can go a long way toward thwarting a hostile act.

The cardinal rule for personal safety is for people to be aware of their surroundings at all times and to observe the behavior of others in the area. However, detecting surveillance — especially when it is performed well — often requires that one take extra precautions. One of the best ways for a person to determine whether he or she is being tailed is to use a surveillance detection route (SDR). By altering their behavior, those under surveillance can manipulate the situation, causing members of the surveillance team to act in ways that betray their presence and intentions. In fact, understanding that a potential victim can manipulate a surveillance situation is one of the most important lessons to be gleaned from this series.

Although hiring professional surveillance detection and countersurveillance teams — or drivers trained to provide more than a smooth ride — are obvious choices, not everyone who is at risk has the resources to do so. Individuals, however, can take a number of steps to determine whether they are under hostile surveillance. Techniques for manipulating surveillance teams include stair-stepping, varying routes and departure times, using intrusion points, and timing stops.

The most common and effective SDR tool is the channel — a long, straight corridor that has several exits or routes at the far end. A person who wants to ensure he is not being tailed can use the channel to force the surveillant to follow closely behind. This is because the operative cannot parallel the subject's route and cannot know which way the subject will go at the end of the channel. Natural channels are long narrow bridges and sections of highway that have no exits or overpasses, but that branch out in a number of routes on the far side. The subway is also a type of channel. Most people likely use such channels in their daily routes but are unaware of them.

Stair-stepping involves making turns — in a vehicle or on foot — that deviate slightly from the most direct route to the destination. During a stair-stepping sequence, a surveillant is likely to reveal his presence by staying with his subject during the series of turns — a common mistake among amateur surveillance operatives who fear losing sight of the target. The subject, however, should not make sudden, unnatural movements, or the surveillance team will break off without revealing its presence.

By varying routes and departure times, the subject can cause surveillants to go into action abruptly in order to compensate for the change in plans. Unless it has a wide area covered, the team could be forced to break off surveillance or act more overtly to prevent losing its target. Varying departure times from fixed locations such as the home or office also can be quite effective because it can force the surveillants to remain in one place longer than anticipated — and thus attract attention.

An intrusion point is a place along a person's route, preferably with a secondary exit such as a back door, where a surveillance target can stop and see whether anyone is following. If the intrusion point has a secondary exit, the subject can give the surveillance team the slip by heading out the back door. If the surveillance team knows the place, however, it could very well have another surveillant waiting by the secondary exit. This kind of coverage generally requires the kind of resources that only a government can lavish on a surveillance operation. Intrusion points — like all parts of the SDR — cannot be random. They should be planned in advance and worked into a daily routine.

Finally, conducting timing stops is one more way to spot hostile surveillance. A timing stop is a place where a person stops and looks back before reaching the final destination to ensure he is not being tailed. It doesn't have to be long — especially in a vehicle.

Physical threats to individuals from terrorists, assassins, kidnappers or even stalkers are site-dependant. The assailants choose the location and timing of their attack based on criteria that gives them the best chance of successfully carrying out the attack and — unless the attacker is mentally disturbed or on a suicide mission — of escaping. These criteria include restricting or controlling the target's ability to maneuver or escape, and providing optimal cover for any surveillance or attack team.

Another way to safeguard against potential hazards is by conducting an analysis of one's normal route to identify points of vulnerability such as overpasses, bridges and tunnels, to minimize hazards and deny potential attackers any advantage. Route analysis can also identify potential attack sites — points along the route that restrict the target's movement, and provide cover and an escape route for the attackers. Once a potential attack site is identified, possible vantage points — or perches — for hostile surveillance or attack teams should be watched.

High-profile individuals or anyone who resides in a high-crime or high-terrorism area such as Mexico City or Baghdad should take the initiative and identify surveillants before they have the opportunity to strike. Once hostile surveillance has been identified, immediate action should be taken and assistance called in.

# CHAPTER 3:
# PROTECTING PEOPLE

---

## Bhutto's Death: Fatal Factors
### *Dec. 28, 2007*

A day after the assassination of former Pakistani Prime Minister Benazir Bhutto, the precise details of the attack are still murky, but the picture of what happened is clearer than it was yesterday. First of all, reports from knowledgeable sources now indicate that Bhutto died from head trauma caused either by the explosive device or by striking her head on the hatch of her vehicle and not from bullet wounds, as previously reported. This is an important distinction, because the set of skills and level of training required to accurately shoot at a moving target through a heavy crowd while being jostled — and successfully hit that target with multiple rounds — is very different from the skill set required to merely push the button on a suicide vest. The former scenario requires a far higher level of professionalism than the latter.

Indeed, if these newer reports are accurate, they would indicate that the attack that took Bhutto's life was not all that different in concept or skill level from the Oct. 18 attempt on her life. This would reinforce the theory that a militant Islamist group was responsible for the attack and lend credence to the purported al Qaeda statement claiming responsibility for Bhutto's death.

The attempt to assassinate Bhutto really came as no surprise. Bhutto and her party had received many threats and warnings, and many of these had even been made publicly. Of course, the Oct. 18 suicide attack against her slow-moving procession upon her return to Pakistan was in many ways the loudest warning of all, though STRATFOR had received reports from people close to Bhutto that there had been several other attempts since then that had been foiled by her security team.

Given this general atmosphere, it is interesting to note the ways the operation that succeeded in assassinating Bhutto was greatly aided by the actions of the politician, her followers and her security team. First, given that it was a political necessity for Bhutto to attend the rally at the Liaqat Bagh Park, her security team should have been on its toes, since her presence gave the people who wanted to kill her a set place and time to act. They knew where she was going to be and when. Second, the physical layout of the park itself ensured that there were only a limited number of entrances to the facility. These entrances served as choke points; Bhutto had to pass through one of them to enter and exit the park. It is not known if Bhutto's motorcade used the same entrance to enter and exit, but chances are that it did enter and exit via the back gate — especially given the throng of people who attended the rally and who likely jammed the main entrance road. It is also probable that every VIP who visits that park uses the back entrance gate.

This is where protective intelligence would have been particularly useful in identifying the potential hazards presented by the choke-point of the rear gate, causing the executive protection team to pay particular attention to that spot. Security officers traditionally like to do two things when faced with a choke point they must traverse: control it and monitor activity there and get through it as quickly as possible. In the Bhutto case, neither of these was done. The area around the rear gate was not controlled; it can be seen in photos taken right before the attack that Bhutto's supporters clogged the road at that point, forcing the executive protection team to dismount from their vehicles and "run the fenders" in an effort to keep people off Bhutto's vehicle and attempt to clear the way in front of the vehicle so that it could move forward.

It is important to remember that there is no such thing as a bomb-and-bullet-proof vehicle. Even main battle tanks are vulnerable to mines, rockets and improvised explosive devices. Because of this, it is very important for protective motorcades to keep moving; they are vulnerable when they are stationary or barely moving, as Bhutto's motorcade was as it left the park's back entrance. During this very vulnerable time, Bhutto did something that is unimaginable from a security officer's viewpoint: She opened the sunroof of the vehicle and stood up to wave to the crowd. This act not only breached the relative safety of the armored vehicle and provided a place into which a grenade or Molotov cocktail could be tossed, but it also exposed her head and most of her torso.

The suicide device that was used against Bhutto does not appear to have been very large, but from the photos of the damage done to the vehicles in the motorcade and to the wounded and killed security officers and bystanders, it does appear to have been packed with shrapnel resembling ball bearings. It also does not appear that the device was detonated in intimate contact with her vehicle, or that her vehicle — which was used to transport her to the hospital — was badly damaged by the blast. Indeed, regardless of whether Bhutto was killed by shrapnel or by striking her head on the hatch of her vehicle, had she kept her head and torso completely inside the vehicle, she very well might have survived this attempt as she did the last.

We do not know why Bhutto's security team allowed her to expose herself at such a particularly vulnerable point in time and space, or if they even objected to her decision to do so, but it is very likely that in the end, political considerations and personal preference trumped security concerns, and it was these political considerations that contributed greatly to Bhutto's death.

It is an unfortunate fact that in the security business, security officers are frequently ignored — and often fired — by powerful and strong-willed individuals who fail to heed their security advice. Frankly, some protectees live in a state of denial and are slow to acknowledge that anyone would want to harm them. This fact is even more pronounced in developing countries where security officers tend to be poorly trained, hail from the lower class and are generally not well regarded by society or even their protectees. In many cases, even when security officers have the training and background to realize something is dangerous they can be powerless to stop their protectee from making a fatal error.

The circumstances surrounding Bhutto's death could also have been complicated by the actions of her security team if — and this is a big if — a member of the team grabbed her and forced her down into the vehicle after shots were fired. It could have been this action that resulted in her hitting her head on the hatch and not the force of the explosion. It will be most interesting to keep an eye on the investigation surrounding this death in an attempt to further clarify the chain of fatal factors that led to Bhutto's assassination.

## India: A Kidnapping Case Study
### *Jan. 29, 2008*

A special police force rescued the president of an Indian pharmaceutical company who was abducted along a highway in India's Madhya Pradesh state on Jan. 18 and held for nine days. Ashwtini Bhatt, president of Nicholas Piramal India Ltd., and his driver were abducted by a group of armed men while traveling to Indore from Gwalior, where Bhatt had just attended an investment meeting with government officials.

Kidnapping in India is nothing new. In fact, according to some estimates, India now ranks among the top 10 countries in the world for kidnapping threats. The tactics used in this latest reported incident demonstrate how some basic security measures can help mitigate this threat.

# KIDNAPPING OF ASHWTINI BHATT IN JANUARY 2008

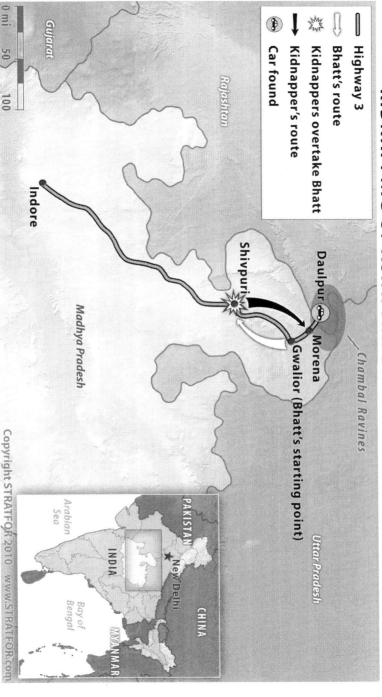

Highway 3
Bhatt's route
Kidnappers overtake Bhatt
Kidnapper's route
Car found

Gujarat

Rajasthan

Madhya Pradesh

Indore

Shivpuri

Daulpur

Morena

Gwalior (Bhatt's starting point)

Chambal Ravines

Uttar Pradesh

0 mi    50    100

PAKISTAN

INDIA

Arabian
Sea

New Delhi

CHINA

MYANMAR

Bay of
Bengal

Following his rescue, Bhatt said that about 30 minutes after leaving Gwalior, he and his driver were overtaken by a vehicle and then forced to stop as they were traveling on a highway near Shivpuri, a deserted area that borders the states of Rajasthan, Uttar Pradesh and Madhya Pradesh. The area is known for having little police presence and for being home to a variety of criminal groups. The victims were then forced into another vehicle and driven to a nearby village in the Chambal ravines, where they were blindfolded and forced to walk several hours to yet another village. There they were held in a small room for the remainder of their captivity.

The fact that Bhatt was attending a scheduled event and was abducted shortly after leaving the meeting suggests that this was not a random abduction and that the kidnappers had conducted surveillance on Bhatt. The kidnappers would have planned the abduction to take place in an area that would maximize their control of the situation.

The planning stage is a prime time to detect a developing threat. A protection detail — or even an observant individual — practicing protective intelligence in this case would have had the opportunity to observe suspicious behavior prior to the abduction.

Police reported that one group performed the actual abduction and then handed the victims off to a second group that transported them to a safe-house and was responsible for guarding them. A third group would have been responsible for surveilling the victims. These reports that various cells of the group were dedicated to certain parts of the abduction suggest that the kidnapping gang is fairly experienced.

This case also raises the issue of Indian security forces' capabilities in responding to kidnappings. It reportedly took up to a week for Madhya Pradesh police to locate the victims, tracing a telephone that the kidnappers used to demand ransom. Police said that when they arrived at the village, several armed men fled the area where they found Bhatt and his driver. Several suspects guarding the hostages were taken into custody, though these members of the gang would be the easiest to replace. The surveillance and grab teams — which were not arrested — are likely more sophisticated and experienced.

Nevertheless, it is significant that law enforcement succeeded in rescuing the victims without a ransom being paid. Criminal organizations such as these are primarily profit-driven and nearly always conduct a cost-benefit analysis. If law enforcement is able to thwart kidnapping gangs and prevent them from getting paid, criminal groups can be expected to switch to crimes with a more certain return for their efforts and risks.

---

# China: Security Aspects of the Dalai Lama's Travels
## *March 25, 2008*

The Dalai Lama, the spiritual leader of Tibet, frequently travels abroad from his base in India for teaching, speeches and political interaction. During 2008 he is currently scheduled to visit the United States, United Kingdom, Germany, France and Australia.

With protests and riots in Tibet and western China, and political tensions rising between China and other nations over Beijing's handling of the Tibet situation, his visits this year — particularly those ahead of the Beijing Olympics — could represent a greater security issue for the Dalai Lama than usual.

Chinese officials have portrayed the violence in Tibet and surrounding provinces as the direct result of the Dalai Lama's actions. Beijing has hinted at an international conspiracy backing the so-called "Dalai Lama Clique" to create discord in China and undermine the Communist Party and China's territorial integrity. While few foreigners accept China's characterization of the Dalai Lama as a terrorist mastermind, many countries' governments will take Chinese political sensitivities into account before allowing a visit by the Dalai Lama or arranging meetings between political leaders and the Tibetan spiritual leader.

The Dalai Lama's travel schedule already is raising political issues with China and in the countries in question. British Prime Minister

Gordon Brown has said he will meet with the Dalai Lama during the Tibetan leader's May visit — a political imperative to demonstrate that Brown is not giving into Chinese pressures and ignoring human and religious rights issues in China during the Olympic year. Beijing has criticized the planned meeting. More meetings with political leaders in other countries on the Dalai Lama's itinerary are likely, as leaders will want to demonstrate that their respective trips to Beijing for the Olympics do not mean they are ignoring human rights issues in China.

The Dalai Lama does not pay only state visits, however. Most of his travels are to spiritual centers and universities for speeches and teaching. Security at these venues is not nearly as robust as security on a presidential or prime ministerial visit — though he will be protected by the State Department's Diplomatic Security Service on the U.S. leg of his travels. The Dalai Lama could face a heightened threat this year at these less secure venues.

Beijing has portrayed the violence in Tibet as stemming from separatist ethnic Tibetan militants and criminals fighting the majority ethnic Han Chinese. While Beijing has tempered this with pictures of some Tibetans helping the Han during the riots in Lhasa to prevent vigilante action by the Han against the Tibetans, there are already reports of Hui (Muslim Han, a large component of the Han settlers in Tibet) carrying out attacks on Tibetans.

Chinese media have emphasized the deaths of Han Chinese shopkeepers, particularly women, who died when their stores were ransacked and set ablaze. These are emotionally charged images that could trigger violent responses inside China. But they might also stir up ethnic nationalist Chinese sentiments abroad, raising the specter of an individual or small group plotting to assassinate the Dalai Lama during his travels. From a protective intelligence perspective, such lone-wolf operations are often difficult to predict and defend against, particularly as the Dalai Lama will be attending numerous public functions. Accordingly, there also will be a high probability of demonstrations and potential bomb threats during the Dalai Lama's travels.

# The U.S. Election Season: Security Challenges and Conventional Wisdom
## *March 26, 2008*

As the struggle grinds on in the United States for the Democratic presidential nomination, it appears there will be no clear winner before the Democratic National Convention begins Aug. 25 in Denver, Colo. This contest of firsts — the first female presidential candidate in Hillary Clinton and the first African-American candidate to win so many primaries and delegates in Barack Obama — has been hard-fought, and likely will become even more heated between now and the convention.

The Obama campaign has leveled claims of racism over remarks made by former President Bill Clinton before the January South Carolina primary, and more recently over the widely publicized comments by Geraldine Ferraro, who was forced to resign from the Clinton campaign. The Obama campaign also has had to face racism charges over controversial comments made from the pulpit by Obama's longtime friend and pastor, the Rev. Jeremiah Wright, who until February was pastor of the Trinity United Church of Christ in Chicago.

From a security perspective, each election cycle brings huge challenges. The task of protecting presidential candidates has grown ever larger as campaigns and primary elections have been pushed ever earlier. In fact, when Obama received U.S. Secret Service (USSS) protection in May 2007, he made history by being the candidate to receive USSS protection the earliest. Much of the rationale behind the decision to provide Obama with protection so early was based on the conventional wisdom that radical white racists would seek to harm him. A review of several radical white racist Web sites, however, shows that many radical white racists would prefer that Obama be elected, rather than Clinton or Republican candidate John McCain, both of whom they consider to be controlled by Jewish interest groups. Perhaps the greatest threat to all three of the candidates — as is nearly always the case — would be a mentally disturbed lone gunman, and such a person could choose to target any of the candidates for any number of reasons.

## Challenges

Major presidential candidates have been afforded USSS protection since the 1968 assassination of Robert Kennedy at the site of a campaign event. Presidential elections give the USSS and other security personnel headaches for a number of reasons. Foremost among them is the fact that campaigns are, by their very nature, fast, furious and geographically diverse. In the run-up to an important primary — or on a day like Super Tuesday, when there are multiple primaries — candidates can hopscotch across a state or even across the country. Candidates' schedules often are packed with events that start before sunrise and last until long after dark, and each of the events on that very full schedule requires a great deal of security planning and preparation. Each site on the candidate's itinerary must first be visited by a security advance team or agent, who will survey the site, gather all the details of the event and then create a plan, called a security survey, for the measures to be put in place for the event. In the case of a 10-minute stop at a diner, for example, the plan can simply outline which entrance should be used and how the agents should be deployed, as well as provide emergency evacuation procedures. Such small events often can be handled by the security detail itself, as are most of the impromptu stops and events. In general, the threat is smaller at an impromptu stop than it is at a planned event because the spontaneous nature of the impromptu stop does not give potential malefactors the opportunity to make attack plans. Large, well-publicized events, on the other hand, can provide ample opportunity to plan an attack, and because of this they require additional security measures.

In the case of a large planned function, security measures can be expanded to include bomb sweeps, access control and screening, counter-sniper coverage, sweeps for hazardous materials, etc. Any event that is swept for bombs by an explosive ordnance disposal team must then be watched, or "posted," for the entire period between the sweep and the event. Advance work, pre-posting, close protection, protective intelligence, liaison with local and state police agencies and access control all require bodies. Consider the manpower required to secure one such event, multiply that by several similar events daily and by the number of candidates being protected — and then spread it over a period of many months — and it becomes apparent why the USSS, with its 3,200 special agents and 1,200 uniformed officers, is hard-pressed during an election season. At the same time, the USSS must also maintain its normal protective coverage of the sitting president and vice president, first lady, former presidents and first ladies and visiting heads of state. In fact, the USSS frequently lacks the manpower for all of these functions and often will borrow special agents from the Bureau of Alcohol, Tobacco, Firearms and Explosives and the Internal Revenue Service, or deputies from the U.S. Marshals Service.

Another challenge during election season is the fact that candidates are compelled to meet and greet supporters, kiss babies and press the flesh, which means they need to enter crowds. This is the aspect of the job that protection agents most abhor, because danger can lurk anywhere in a crowd. The density of a crowd makes it very difficult for agents to see bulges and bumps that can indicate that a person is armed. Moreover, the sheer number of people makes it difficult for agents to spot individuals who are behaving abnormally. That said, U.S. protective agencies such as the USSS and the Diplomatic Security Service spend much time and effort training their special agents to "work the crowd." They are the best in the world at it, but that does not mean it is an easy task or one the agents enjoy.

As we have discussed in relation to the two assassination attempts against Pakistani opposition leader Benazir Bhutto, crowds are a security nightmare. This is true anywhere in the world. Indeed, a number of assassins and would-be assassins in the United States have struck from crowds. President William McKinley was greeting a crowd at an exposition in Buffalo, N.Y., in 1901, when he was shot by anarchist

Leon Frank Czolgosz, who had concealed a revolver in a handkerchief. Presidential candidate George Wallace was shot in 1972 by Arthur Bremer, who emerged from a crowd during a campaign stop in Laurel, Md. Wallace survived the attempt, but the attack left him disabled for life. Lynette "Squeaky" Fromme and Sarah Jane Moore both attempted to assassinate President Gerald Ford from crowds in September 1975. John Hinckley also used a crowd of reporters (an area known as the press pen) as camouflage in his 1981 assassination attempt against President Ronald Reagan. In the past, one radical group threatened to stab politicians working the crowds with HIV-infected needles, and other groups have plotted to attack prominent politicians with toxins such as ricin.

### Conventional Wisdom

At present, the conventional wisdom holds that Obama, as an African-American, is under a greater threat than either Clinton or McCain. However, a close look at the rhetoric on many radical white racist Web sites reveals a couple of things that appear to contradict the conventional wisdom. In fact, the rhetoric seems to indicate that all three remaining candidates are at risk. First, many people who post comments on these types of sites believe the real problem is not African-Americans but Jews, who they believe are using African-Americans as a tool to oppress white Americans. In other words, they see African-Americans as a symptom of a larger Jewish problem. They believe that a cabal of Jews — an entity they call the Zionist Occupation Government (ZOG) — secretly controls the U.S. government. They further believe that both McCain and Clinton are totally controlled by the ZOG, and that the ZOG will oppose Obama because he is not toeing the line. Using the logic that an Obama victory would be bad for the ZOG, these racists would rather see Obama get elected than either the "ZOG-controlled" Clinton or McCain.

Many of these same radical white racists also believe that Obama is a godsend to them. First, they believe that if he is defeated in either the primaries or the general election, it will spark huge riots in inner cities across the United States — riots that, they say, will demonstrate the "true nature" of African-Americans. Even if Obama is elected, many white racists believe he will behave in a manner that will inflame racial tensions, causing a polarization that will assist them in their recruiting efforts and ultimately in their fight to wrest control of the United States from the ZOG. Of course, some white racists also say they hope a lone wolf will assassinate Obama in an effort to spark a race war. This is the reason he is under USSS protection.

But Obama is not the only candidate at risk from right-wing extremists. In addition to the white racists who believe McCain and Clinton are Jewish puppets, there are other right-wing radicals who are unhappy with both McCain and Clinton over their respective stances on immigration. Right-wing radicals also were not fond of the Bill Clinton presidency. When they discuss the prospects of a Hillary Clinton presidency, they frequently refer to people such as former Attorney General Janet Reno and incidents such as the Waco siege and the air campaign against Serbia.

All of the presidential candidates also face the threat of a mentally disturbed lone wolf, like Hinckley or Bremer. Such individuals have long posed one of the most severe threats to prominent individuals in the United States.

McCain also has the additional threats of radical leftists who oppose his stance on the war in Iraq, though frankly they are more likely to embarrass him than seriously harm him. Of more concern is the real threat posed by radical , of both the jihadist and Hezbollah variety, who see McCain's stance on the war in Iraq, his unequivocal support of Israel and his tough rhetoric toward Iran as threatening.

Any election season poses difficult security challenges for the USSS, but the unique circumstances of this year's election are making the job especially tough on the already overtaxed protection service.

# Mexico: Examining the Cartel War through a Protective Lens
### *May 14, 2008*

Mexico's long and violent drug cartel war has recently intensified. The past week witnessed the killings of no fewer than six senior police officials, one of whom was Edgar Millan Gomez, acting head of the Mexican Federal Police and the highest-ranking federal cop in Mexico. Millan Gomez was shot to death May 8 just after entering his home in Mexico City.

Within the past few days, six suspects have been arrested in connection with his murder. One of the ringleaders is said to be a former federal highway police officer. The suspects appear to have ties to the Sinaloa cartel. In fact, Millan Gomez was responsible for a police operation in January that led to the arrest of Alfredo Beltran Leyva, the cartel's second-in-command. Mexican police believe Beltran Leyva's brother, Arturo (who is also a significant player in the Sinaloa cartel structure), commissioned the hit.

During the same time period, violence from the cartel war has visited the family of Joaquin "El Chapo" Guzman Loera, the Sinaloa cartel leader who has the distinction of being Mexico's most-wanted drug kingpin. On May 8, Guzman Loera's son, Edgar Guzman Beltran, and two companions were killed by a large-scale ambush as they left a shopping mall in Culiacan, Sinaloa.

In addition to discussing the geopolitical implications of this escalation in the violence, we thought it would be instructive to look at the recent wave of violence through the lens of protective intelligence. This will not only allow us to see what lessons can be learned from the attacks but also provide insight on how similar attacks can be avoided in the future, which is the real aim of protective intelligence.

## Tactical Details of the Recent Attacks

On the evening of May 1, Roberto Velasco Bravo, director of investigations against organized crime for Mexico's state public security police (SSP), was gunned down as he returned to his Mexico City home. Two assailants reportedly approached Velasco Bravo as he parked his sport utility vehicle and shot him in the head at close range before fleeing the scene. Although the incident initially was believed to have been a robbery attempt gone bad, the discovery of a .380-caliber handgun fitted with a suppressor near the crime scene suggests the shooting was actually a professionally targeted assassination. Local press also reported that Velasco Bravo died on his day off and that his bodyguard had been ordered to stand down because he was planning to travel outside the city.

On May 2, less than 24 hours after the Velasco Bravo shooting, inspector Jose Aristeo Gomez Martinez, the administrative director of the Federal Preventative Police (PFP), was gunned down in front of his home in the wealthy Coyoacan neighborhood of Mexico City. Gomez Martinez and a woman were talking in front of the house around midnight when two armed men surprised them and reportedly attempted to force Gomez Martinez into the back seat of his own car. Gomez Martinez struggled with the men and was shot in the arm and chest. Mexican authorities say the motive for the Gomez Martinez killing remains murky. However, the circumstances surrounding the case — he was shot with a suppressed .380 pistol outside of his residence — are certainly very similar to the Velasco Bravo and Millan Gomez killings.

In the Millan Gomez attack, alleged members of a murder-for-hire gang shot and killed the federal police chief as he returned to his home in the early hours of the morning. Millan Gomez was reportedly shot eight times at close range by a gunman armed with two handguns — one of which was a .380 with a suppressor. The gunman was reportedly waiting inside Millan Gomez's apartment building. The victim apparently struggled with his assailant and attempted to grab the suppressed weapon from the gunman. During the struggle, the gunman reportedly shot Millan Gomez in the hand once with the suppressed weapon and then several times in the torso with his back-up weapon, which was not suppressed. Millan Gomez's two-man protection team, who had just dropped him off at the door, heard the nonsuppressed shots and returned to the apartment building to investigate. One member of the protection team was wounded in the chest by the fleeing gunman, but the team was able to wound and apprehend him alive. The interrogation of the gunman and the investigation of the equipment and other items found in his possession led to the recent arrest of the five other suspects allegedly tied to the assassination gang.

Also on May 8, Edgar Guzman Beltran, the son of Sinaloa cartel leader Joaquin "El Chapo" Guzman Loera, was killed at 8:50 p.m. local time in Culiacan, Sinaloa state. Guzman Beltran was leaving a local shopping mall with two friends — one of whom was Arturo Meza Cazares, the son of Blanca Margarita Cazares Salazar, reputed to be the cartel's top money launderer — when the three were caught in a heavy hail of gunfire. Reports from the scene indicate that the team that attacked Guzman Beltran may have involved as many as 40 gunmen from a rival cartel who opened up on the three men with AK-47 rifles and a rocket-propelled grenade launcher. Other reports put the number of ambushers at around 20. In any event, even 20 men armed with AKs and a rocket-propelled grenade launcher is a significant force, and something one would expect to see in a war zone such as Iraq or Afghanistan rather than in Mexico.

On May 9, Esteban Robles Espinosa, commander of Mexico City's investigative police force, was attacked by a group of armed men shortly after he left his house at about 8:30 a.m. Four gunmen traveling in a truck and another in a compact car opened fire on him at an intersection near his home. The attack appears to be a classic vehicular ambush involving a blocking vehicle and an assault team. Robles Espinosa apparently attempted to avoid the attack and flee the site, but his escape attempt ended when his vehicle struck a tree. Robles Espinosa was shot seven times — four times in the throat, once in the neck, and twice in the head. He died shortly after arriving at a hospital. Authorities reportedly found 20 casings from 9mm and .40-caliber cartridges at the scene of the attack. The placement of the shots in this case appears to be uncharacteristically controlled for Mexico, where victims are normally wounded in various parts of their bodies. The concentration of wounds in the head and neck would appear to indicate that at least one of the shooters was an accomplished marksman. The shot placement might also indicate that Robles Espinosa was wearing a protective vest, and the assailants, being aware of the vest, directed their fire toward his head.

## Common Themes

The Millan Gomez, Velasco Bravo and Gomez Martinez shootings were all similar in that they involved suppressed .380 handguns and were intended to be clean and discreetly conducted events. They stand in stark contrast to many of the cartel killings in Mexico, which tend to be more like the killings of Beltran Guzman and involve massive firepower and very little precision or discretion. Even though the Millan Gomez killing got messy, and the shooter was caught, it was intended to be a very quiet, surgical hit — until Murphy's law kicked in for the assassin.

It is notable that the killing of the four police officials all occurred in proximity to their homes, and that all four attacks were conducted during an arrival or departure at the home. It has long been common for terrorists and criminal kidnappers or assassins to focus on the home or office of their prospective target because these are known locations that the potential victim frequently visits with some regularity. Also, homes are often preferable to offices because they usually have less security, and criminals or terrorists can operate around them more easily and with less chance of being caught. Arrivals and departures are prime times for attacks because the target is generally easier to locate and quickly acquire when on foot or in a car than when in a building.

Furthermore, the objective of pre-operational surveillance is to detect the target's patterns and vulnerabilities so that an attack can be planned. Historically, one of the most likely times for an attack to occur is when a potential victim is leaving from or returning to a known location. The most predictable move traditionally is the home-to-office move; however, the team that conducted the surveillance on Velasco Bravo, Gomez Martinez and Millan Gomez apparently found them to be predictable in their evening moves and planned the attacks accordingly. Robles Espinosa was attacked during the more-stereotypical morning move. Attacking in the evening could also give the assailants the cover of darkness. The low-key assassination cell behind the Velasco Bravo, Gomez Martinez and Millan Gomez attacks seemed to prefer that kind of cover. It is also possible that in the Guzman Beltran case, the shopping mall was a known place for him to frequent and that he had established a pattern of visiting there in the evening.

All five of the attacks also occurred in close proximity to vehicles. Millan Gomez, Gomez Martinez and Guzman Beltran were attacked while outside their vehicles; Robles Espinosa and Vellasco Bravo were attacked while in theirs, though neither of the men had an armored vehicle.

## Protective Intelligence Lessons

A former federal police officer was arrested in connection with the Millan Gomez case, and he was found to have a list of license plates and home addresses. Such information alone, however, is not enough to plan an assassination. Extensive pre-operational surveillance is also required. From the careful planning of the Velasco Bravo, Gomez Martinez and Millan Gomez hits, it is apparent that the targets were under surveillance for a prolonged period of time. The fact that Robles Espinosa was hit during his morning move from home to work also suggests he had an established pattern that had been picked up by surveillance. Even for hits like the Guzman Beltran killing, one does not amass a team of 20 or 40 assassins at the drop of a hat. Clearly, the operation was planned and the target had been watched.

The fact that surveillance was conducted in each of these cases means that the people conducting that surveillance were forced to expose themselves to detection. Furthermore, pre-operational surveillance is normally not that sophisticated, since people rarely look for it. This means that, had countersurveillance been conducted, these efforts likely would have been detected, especially since countersurveillance often focuses on known, predictable locations such as the home and office.

Another important lesson is that bodyguards and armored cars are no guarantee of protection in and of themselves. Assailants can look for and exploit vulnerabilities — as they did in the Velasco Bravo and Millan Gomez cases — if they are allowed to conduct surveillance at will and are given the opportunity to thoroughly assess the protective security program. Even if there are security measures in place, malefactors may choose to attack in spite of security and, in such a case, will do so with adequate resources to overcome those security measures. If there are protective agents, the attackers will plan to neutralize them first. If there is an armored vehicle, they will find ways to defeat the armor — something easily accomplished with the rocket-propelled grenades, LAW rockets and .50-caliber sniper rifles found in the arsenals of Mexican cartels.

Unfortunately, many people believe that the presence of armed bodyguards — or armed guards combined with armored vehicles — provides absolute security. This macho misconception is not confined to Latin America but is pervasive there. Frankly, when we consider the size of the assault team employed in the Guzman Beltran hit (even if it consisted of only 20 men) and their armaments, there are very few protective details in the world sufficiently trained and equipped to deal with that level of threat. Executive protection teams and armored cars provide very little protection against dozens of attackers armed with AK rifles and rocket-propelled grenades, especially if the attackers are given free rein to conduct surveillance and plan their attack.

Indeed, many people — including police and executive protection personnel — either lack or fail to employ good observation skills.

These skills are every bit as important as marksmanship — if not more — but are rarely taught or practiced. Additionally, even if a protection agent observes something unusual, in many cases there is no system in place to record these observations and no efficient way to communicate them or to compare them to the observations of others. There is often no process to investigate such observations to determine if they are indicators of something untoward.

The real counter to such a threat is heightened security awareness and a robust countersurveillance program, coupled with careful route and schedule analysis. Routes and traveling times must be varied, surveillance must be looked for and those conducting surveillance must not be afforded the opportunity to operate at will. Suspicious events must be catalogued and investigated. Emphasis must also be placed on attack recognition and driver training to provide every possibility of spotting a pending attack and avoiding it before it can be successfully launched. Action is always faster than reaction. And even a highly-skilled protection team can be defeated if the attacker gains the tactical element of surprise — especially if coupled with overwhelming firepower.

Ideally, those conducting surveillance must be made uncomfortable, or even manipulated into revealing their positions, when it proves advantageous to countersurveillance teams. Dummy motorcade moves are a fine tool to add to the mix, as is the use of safe houses for alternate residences and offices. Any ploy to confuse, deceive or deter potential scouts that would ultimately make them tip their hand are valuable tricks of the trade employed by protective intelligence practitioners — professionals tasked with the difficult mission of deterring the type of assassinations we have recently seen in Mexico.

# Mexico: Tactical Implications of the Labastida Killing
## *June 27, 2008*

The brazen killing of Igor Labastida Calderon, a commander of the traffic and contraband division in Mexico's Federal Preventive Police, carries important tactical lessons that must be learned if Mexican authorities are to have any hope of keeping any of their charges safe.

Labastida was killed while eating lunch at a restaurant in the Mexican capital. He was accompanied by his bodyguard (who was also killed) and several other police agents, three of whom were wounded in the attack.

The modus operandi in the Labastida assassination stands in stark contrast to the May killings of Edgar Millan Gomez, Roberto Velasco Bravo and Jose Aristeo Gomez Martinez. In each of those three cases, the victims were shot after dark with suppressed .380 pistols and had no executive protection agents present. (Millan Gomez's protective agents had just dropped him off at the door of his residence; they returned to the scene after the shooting and subdued the shooter after Millan Gomez struggled with his assailant, forcing him to fire shots from a second, non-suppressed weapon.) In spite of the foul-up in the Millan Gomez hit, these three operations were designed to be discreet and cleanly conducted.

By killing Labastida Calderon — who was investigating the Millan Gomez killing — the cartel honcho behind it (most likely Arturo Beltran Levya) was sending a message, namely, if you investigate me, you will die. The killing also was designed intentionally to send a second message: I can get you any time and any place regardless of protection, and you cannot stop me.

In spite of the different modi operandi between this case and the killings last month, a tactical analysis of the Labastida killing reveals certain similarities. In all these cases, the killers had good intelligence (some of which came from inside sources). Perhaps more important, the killers had the freedom to conduct pre-operational surveillance and plan the assassination without detection or hindrance. Obviously, had their surveillance been detected, additional security measures would have been implemented. As it was, the surveillance was not detected, and the assailants were able to launch the attack and gain tactical surprise on Labastida and his security detail.

The tactical lessons to be taken from this case are very similar to those drawn from the assassinations last month and apparently not heeded.

- Attackers cannot be permitted free rein to conduct surveillance. Had countersurveillance efforts been employed, the target's security details probably would have detected the assailants.

- Personal information of potential targets, such as schedules, must be carefully guarded.

- Large men with large guns and armored cars are no guarantee of protection in and of themselves. Assailants can — and will — look for and exploit vulnerabilities. Even when there are security measures in place, brazen criminals may choose to attack in spite of security. When they do, they will attack with adequate resources to overcome security measures. If there are protective agents, the attackers will neutralize them first. If there is an armored vehicle, they will find ways to defeat the armor — something easily accomplished with the rocket-propelled grenades (RPGs), LAW rockets and .50-caliber sniper rifles found in the arsenals of Mexican cartels.

- Observation skills and attack recognition are critical. They are literally the difference between life and death.

- VIPs must not wholly rely on their executive protection details to keep them safe. They must take ownership of their own security, even when that means doing uncomfortable things like varying times and routes and not visiting favorite spots on a predictable basis.

As we saw in the May 8 killing of Edgar Guzman Beltran, which was conducted by 40 assailants armed with automatic rifles and RPGs, the cartels can mobilize large, heavily equipped assault teams. There are very few protective details in the world capable of withstanding such an assault once launched. Unless a protective intelligence-focused scheme is employed to protect high-ranking Mexican police officials — an approach that stresses the lessons above — the Mexican government will not be able to protect its own.

## Mexico: The Third War
*Feb. 18, 2009*

Mexico has pretty much always been a rough-and-tumble place. In recent years, however, the security environment has deteriorated rapidly, and parts of the country have become incredibly violent. It is now common to see military weaponry such as fragmentation grenades and assault rifles used almost daily in attacks.

In fact, just last week we noted two separate strings of grenade attacks directed against police in Durango and Michoacan states. In the Michoacan incident, police in Uruapan and Lazaro Cardenas were targeted in three grenade attacks during a 12-hour period. Then on Feb. 17, a major firefight occurred just across the border from the United States in Reynosa, when Mexican authorities attempted to apprehend several armed men seen riding in a vehicle. The men fled to a nearby residence and engaged the pursuing police with gunfire, hand grenades and rocket-propelled grenades (RPGs). After the incident, in which five cartel gunmen were killed and several gunmen, cops, soldiers and civilians were wounded, authorities recovered a 60mm mortar, five RPG rounds and two fragmentation grenades.

Make no mistake, considering the military weapons now being used in Mexico and the number of deaths involved, the country is in the middle of a war. In fact, there are actually three concurrent wars being waged in Mexico involving the Mexican drug cartels. The first is the battle being waged among the various Mexican drug cartels seeking control over lucrative smuggling corridors, called plazas. One such battleground is Ciudad Juarez, which provides access to the Interstate 10, Interstate 20 and Interstate 25 corridors inside the United States. The second battle is being fought between the various cartels and the Mexican government, which is seeking to interrupt smuggling operations, curb violence and bring the cartel members to justice.

Then there is a third war being waged in Mexico, though because of its nature it is a bit more subdued. It does not get the same degree of international media attention generated by the running gun battles and grenade and RPG attacks. However, it is no less real, and in many ways it is more dangerous to innocent civilians (as well as foreign tourists and business travelers) than the pitched battles between the cartels and the Mexican government. This third war is the war being waged on the Mexican population by criminals who may or may not be involved with the cartels. Unlike the other battles, where cartel members or government forces are the primary targets and civilians are only killed as collateral damage, on this battlefront, civilians are squarely in the crosshairs.

## The Criminal Front

There are many different shapes and sizes of criminal gangs in Mexico. While many of them are in some way related to the drug cartels, others have various types of connections to law enforcement — indeed, some criminal groups are composed of active and retired cops. These various types of criminal gangs target civilians in a number of ways, including robbery, burglary, carjacking, extortion, fraud and counterfeiting. But of all the crimes committed by these gangs, perhaps the one that creates the most widespread psychological and emotional damage is kidnapping, which also is one of the most underreported crimes.

There is no accurate figure for the number of kidnappings that occur in Mexico each year. All of the data regarding kidnapping is based on partial crime statistics and anecdotal accounts and, in the end, can produce only best-guess estimates. Despite this lack of hard data, however, there is little doubt — based even on the low end of these estimates — that Mexico has become the kidnapping capital of the world.

One of the difficult things about studying kidnapping in Mexico is that the crime not only is widespread, affecting almost every corner of the country, but it also is executed by a wide range of actors who possess varying levels of professionalism — and very different motives. At one end of the spectrum are the high-end kidnapping gangs that abduct high-net-worth individuals and demand ransoms in the millions of dollars. Such groups employ teams of operatives who carry out specialized tasks such as collecting intelligence, conducting surveillance, snatching the target, negotiating with the victim's family and establishing and guarding the safe houses.

At the other end of the spectrum are gangs that roam the streets and randomly kidnap targets of opportunity. These gangs are generally less professional than the high-end gangs and often will hold a victim for only a short time. In many instances, these groups hold the victim just long enough to use the victim's ATM card to drain his or her checking account, or to receive a small ransom of perhaps several hundred or a few thousand dollars from the family. This type of opportunistic kidnapping is often referred to as an "express kidnapping." Sometimes express kidnapping victims are held in the trunk of a car for the duration of their ordeal, which can sometimes last for days if the victim has a large amount in a checking account and a small daily ATM withdrawal limit. Other times, if an express kidnapping gang discovers it has grabbed a high-value target by accident, the gang will hold the victim longer and demand a much higher ransom. Occasionally, these express kidnapping groups will even "sell" a high-value victim to a more professional kidnapping gang.

Between these extremes there is a wide range of groups that fall somewhere in the middle. These are the groups that might target a bank vice president or branch manager rather than the bank's CEO, or that might kidnap the owner of a restaurant or other small business rather than a wealthy industrialist. The presence of such a broad spectrum of kidnapping groups ensures that almost no segment of the population is immune from the kidnapping threat.

In recent years, the sheer magnitude of the threat in Mexico and the fear it generates has led to a crime called virtual kidnapping. In a virtual kidnapping, the victim is not really kidnapped. Instead, the criminals seek to convince a target's family that a kidnapping has occurred, and then use threats and psychological pressure to force the family to pay a quick ransom. Although virtual kidnapping has been around for several years, unwitting families continue to fall for the scam, which is a source of easy money. Some virtual kidnappings have even been conducted by criminals using telephones inside prisons.

As noted above, the motives for kidnapping vary. Many of the kidnappings that occur in Mexico are not conducted for ransom. Often the drug cartels will kidnap members of rival gangs or government officials in order to torture and execute them. This torture is conducted to extract information, intimidate rivals and, apparently in some cases, just to have a little fun. The bodies of such victims are frequently found beheaded or otherwise mutilated. Other times, cartel gunmen will kidnap drug dealers who are tardy in payments or who refuse to pay the "tax" required to operate in the cartel's area of control.

Of course, cartel gunmen do not kidnap only their rivals or cops. As the cartel wars have heated up, and as drug revenues have dropped due to interference from rival cartels or the government, many cartels have resorted to kidnapping for ransom to supplement their cash flow. Perhaps the most widely known group that is engaging in this is the Arellano Felix Organization (AFO), also known as the Tijuana cartel. The AFO has been reduced to a shadow of its former self, its smuggling operations dramatically impacted by the efforts of the U.S. and Mexican governments, as well as by attacks from other cartels and from an internal power struggle. Because of a steep decrease in smuggling revenues, the group has turned to kidnapping and extortion in order to raise the funds necessary to keep itself alive and to return to prominence as a smuggling organization.

## In the Line of Fire

There is very little chance the Mexican government will be able to establish integrity in its law enforcement agencies, or bring law and order to large portions of the country, any time soon. Official corruption and ineptitude are endemic in Mexico, which means that Mexican citizens and visiting foreigners will have to face the threat of kidnapping for the foreseeable future. We believe that for civilians and visiting foreigners, the threat of kidnapping exceeds the threat of being hit by a stray bullet from a cartel firefight. Indeed, things are deteriorating so badly that even professional kidnapping negotiators, once seen as the key to a guaranteed payout, are now being kidnapped themselves. In an even more incredible twist of irony, anti-kidnapping authorities are being abducted and executed.

This environment — and the concerns it has sparked — has provided huge financial opportunities for the private security industry in Mexico. Armored car sales have gone through the roof, as have the number of uniformed guards and executive protection personnel. In fact, the demand for personnel is so acute that security companies are scrambling to find candidates. Such a scramble presents a host of obvious problems, ranging from lack of qualifications to insufficient vetting. In addition to old-fashioned security services, new security-technology companies are also cashing in on the environment of fear, but even high-tech tracking devices can have significant drawbacks and shortcomings.

For many people, armored cars and armed bodyguards can provide a false sense of security, and technology can become a deadly crutch that promotes complacency and actually increases vulnerability. Physical security measures are not enough. The presence of armed bodyguards — or armed guards combined with armored vehicles — does not provide absolute security. This is especially true in Mexico, where large teams of gunmen regularly conduct crimes using military ordnance. Frankly, there are very few executive protection details in the world that have the training and armament to withstand an assault by dozens of attackers armed with assault rifles and RPGs. Private security guards are frequently overwhelmed by Mexican criminals and either killed or forced to flee for their own safety. As we noted in May 2008 after the assassination of Edgar Millan Gomez, acting head of the Mexican Federal Police and the highest-ranking federal cop in Mexico, physical security measures must be supplemented by situational awareness, countersurveillance and protective intelligence.

Criminals look for and exploit vulnerabilities. Their chances for success increase greatly if they are allowed to conduct surveillance at will and are given the opportunity to thoroughly assess the protective security program. We have seen several cases in Mexico in which the criminals even chose to attack despite security measures. In such cases, criminals attack with adequate resources to overcome existing security. For example, if there are protective agents, the attackers will plan to neutralize them first. If there is an armored vehicle, they will find ways to defeat the armor or grab the target when he or she is outside the vehicle. Because of this, criminals must not be allowed to conduct surveillance at will.

Like many crimes, kidnapping is a process. There are certain steps that must be taken to conduct a kidnapping and certain times during the process when those executing it are vulnerable to detection. While these steps may be condensed and accomplished quite quickly in an ad hoc express kidnapping, they are nonetheless followed. In fact, because of the particular steps involved in conducting a kidnapping, the process is not unlike that followed to execute a terrorist attack. The common steps are target selection, planning, deployment, attack, escape and exploitation.

Like the perpetrators of a terrorist attack, those conducting a kidnapping are most vulnerable to detection when they are conducting surveillance — before they are ready to deploy and conduct their attack. As we've noted several times in past analyses, one of the secrets of countersurveillance is that most criminals are not very good at conducting surveillance. The primary reason they succeed is that no one is looking for them.

Of course, kidnappers are also very obvious once they launch their attack, pull their weapons and perhaps even begin to shoot. By this time, however, it might very well be too late to escape their attack. They will have selected their attack site and employed the forces they believe they need to complete the operation. While the kidnappers could botch their operation and the target could escape unscathed, it is simply not practical to pin one's hopes on that possibility. It is clearly better to spot the kidnappers early and avoid their trap before it is sprung and the guns come out.

We have seen many instances of people in Mexico with armed security being kidnapped, and we believe we will likely see more cases of this in the coming months. This trend is due not only to the presence of highly armed and aggressive criminals and the low quality of some security personnel but also to people placing their trust solely in reactive physical security. Ignoring the very real value of critical, proactive measures such as situational awareness, countersurveillance and protective intelligence can be a fatal mistake.

# CHAPTER 4:  SAFEGUARDING PLACES

---

## Corporate Security: The Technology Crutch
### *Aug. 3, 2006*

The Jewish Federation of Greater Seattle was the scene of a fatal shooting on July 28: One woman was killed and five were wounded by an apparent "lone wolf" gunman. The man arrested and charged in the incident, Naveed Afzal Haq, is an American of Pakistani descent who claimed to have acted because he was "angry at Israel."

An act of violence targeting Jews in the United States as a result of the conflict in the Middle East was predictable. But aside from the human tragedy, one of the most troubling aspects of the shooting is that it occurred at a facility that had addressed safety considerations in the past. The Jewish Federation of Greater Seattle uses cipher locks to restrict unauthorized access, external security gates, bullet-resistant windows and closed- circuit television (CCTV) cameras that provide video coverage of the front lobby. Not surprisingly, employees believed themselves to be safe.

However, it is not uncommon for buildings or offices employing good physical security measures to become backdrops for workplace violence or domestic terrorism. Physical security is important, but it does not automatically transform a "soft" target into a "hard" target. In fact, physical security measures may become a kind of psychological crutch that induces a false sense of security or even complacency — attitudes that add to, rather than reduce, one's vulnerabilities.

## Defeating the System

Like any man-made construct, physical security measures — CCTV coverage, metal detectors, cipher locks and so forth — have finite utility. They serve a valuable purpose in institutional security programs, but an effective security program cannot be limited to these. The technology cannot think or evaluate. It is static and can be observed, learned and even fooled. Also, because some systems frequently produce false alarms, warnings in real danger situations may be brushed aside. Given these shortcomings, it is quite possible for anyone planning an act of violence to map out, quantify and then defeat or bypass physical security devices. However, elaborate planning is not always necessary. Consider the common scenario of a worker on a smoke break who props open an otherwise locked door with a rock or trash can as an example of the "internal defeat" of security measures.

To be effective, physical security devices require human interaction. An alarm is useless if no one responds to it, or if it is not turned on; a lock is ineffective if it is not locked. CCTV cameras are used extensively in corporate office buildings and manufacturing centers, but any corporate security manager will tell you that, in reality, they are far more useful in terms of investigating a theft or act of violence after the fact than in preventing one. This was amply illustrated in the London bombings last July; authorities were able to pull up CCTV footage of the bombers afterward, but the cameras by definition could not identify suspicious activity or key in on the bombers before they killed.

Even businesses or government sites that have established elaborate command centers for monitoring CCTV coverage have found that security personnel can monitor only a limited number of screens effectively — and only for a short time before boredom or distraction sets in. And despite the use of software that helps detect motion in sensitive areas, it is not possible for a single person to effectively monitor all the CCTV feeds from a typical corporate office building — let alone an entire corporate campus — for eight or 10 hours at a stretch.

Likewise, access control devices are great when they are monitored but can be easily defeated if they are not. Tailgating — that is, following someone else through the door of a "secure" facility — is very common in corporate America. This tactic is used frequently by thieves — who make it a point to blend into the environment — in gaining access to office buildings, where they steal computers and other valuables. In some cases, brazen tailgater thieves have been able to steal tens of thousands of dollars worth of equipment — sometimes in one haul, sometimes by hitting the same targets repeatedly over time.

In the case of the Jewish Federation, tailgating was used to gain access — though reports have conflicted as to whether the suspect rushed through the door after an employee used her code to open it, or whether he held a gun to a young girl's head and forced her to open the door for him. Aggressive tailgating has been used in other shootings as well: In February, a former postal worker in Goleta, Calif., followed another vehicle through the gates of a mail distribution center. Once in the parking lot, she got out of her car and shot three employees — then took an ID card from one of her victims, using it to enter the building and continue her rampage.

Though the woman in that case had insider knowledge about the distribution of physical security systems, this information can be gained by outsiders as well, using pre-operational surveillance. For instance, it is clear from the surveillance that al Qaeda suspects ran on several financial buildings in the United States that they took great interest in documenting details of the security measures that were in place — including access control, security procedures and guard coverage and schedules.

In reality, all "attack cycles" — even those used by lone-wolf assailants — follow the same general steps. All criminals — whether stalkers, thieves, lone wolves or militants — engage in pre-operational surveillance, but the length of this phase naturally varies depending on the actor and the circumstances. A purse snatcher might case a potential target for a few seconds while a kidnapping crew might conduct surveillance of a potential target for weeks. The degree of surveillance tradecraft — from very clumsy to highly sophisticated — also will vary widely, depending on the training and street skill the operative possesses.

Perhaps the most crucial point to be made about pre-operational surveillance is that it is the phase when someone with hostile intentions is most apt to be detected — and the point in the attack cycle when potential violence can be most easily disrupted or prevented. But detecting the signs of pre-operational surveillance is a uniquely human ability; it requires both cognition and intuition — analysis, "gut feelings" and rapid responses — for which technology is no substitute.

## Heating Up the Environment

No matter what kinds of physical security measures may be in place for a building, office or other facilities, they are far less likely to be effective if a potential assailant feels free to conduct pre-operational surveillance. The more at ease someone feels trying to identify the physical security systems and procedures in place, the higher the odds that person will find ways to beat the system.

A truly "hard" target is one that couples access controls and cameras with an aggressive, alert attitude and awareness. An effective security program is proactive — focused on recognizing potential threats before they present themselves as active threats. One very effective way to do this is to utilize countersurveillance as an element of a facility's (or executive protection) security plan.

Countersurveillance programs operate on a handful of principles — for example, the concept of vantage points or "perches" and how they can be used by someone conducting surveillance. If "perches" around one's facility are identified and activities at those sites are monitored, potential assailants will be less able to conduct pre-operational surveillance at will — and it is quite possible that attacks can be prevented. Another technique that professionals use is "heating up perches" — or directing attention from visible security assets (for example, having roving guards drive past it periodically).

The point of these and other security techniques is to make anyone who might be planning a crime feel uncomfortable during the pre-operational surveillance phase. If he or she believes they have been "burned" (or caught in the act) of surveillance — even if they have not been — they are likely to seek out an "easier" target, unless there is a compelling reason they are drawn to attack a specific person or facility.

## Grassroots Awareness

Some companies have employed surveillance detection programs with great success. Programs employing specially trained, plain-clothes operatives have identified hostile surveillance by militant groups and prevented attacks. They also have helped companies spot and intercept mentally disturbed people, sex offenders and others, such as "tailgating" thieves and car thieves. Uniformed guards who have been trained in surveillance detection for counterterrorism purposes also have proved skillful in detecting and catching criminals.

However, corporate security officers and uniformed guards have only so many eyes and can be in only so many places at once. Thus, proactive security programs also teach the importance of fostering broad security awareness among employees. The training should not leave workers scared or paranoid — just more observant. They need to be trained to look for people who are out of place and who could be surveillants or criminals. They also need to be mindful of people who might be attempting to tailgate into a facility. Most importantly, employees need to know what to do if they see something suspicious and who to call to report it.

As a part of security training, companies should instruct workers on procedures to follow if a shooter enters the building. These "shooter" drills should be practiced regularly — just like a fire, tornado or earthquake drill.

## The Odds

The law of averages indicates that, in all probability, most office buildings or companies will never fall victim to a terrorist attack or workplace violence. However, we strongly believe that the Israel-Hezbollah conflict is likely to spark more attacks like the one in Seattle — and that a few scattered targets in the United States will be affected. Obviously, predicting precise locales or targets is impossible from a distance, but certain classes of likely targets can be identified — such as Israeli diplomatic targets, high-profile organizations that are connected to Israel, prominent Jewish citizens, Jewish-owned businesses, community organizations and religious sites. By the same token, retaliatory violence — possibly targeting Muslim groups or mosques — cannot be ruled out. For either group, we advise putting countermeasures into place, drafting emergency action plans and rehearsing react drills.

As we have noted previously, organizations and businesses tend to increase their funding for security measures in the wake of attacks like that in Seattle. As more attention is devoted to security budgets, considered attention to the effectiveness of specific measures and the value of proactive security training possibly will follow.

---

# Incident Foreshadows Future Attacks in Pakistan
*June 12, 2008*

In a June 10 press conference, Rehman Malik, the internal affairs adviser to Pakistan's prime minister, reported that a suicide bombing plot had been thwarted when Pakistani authorities arrested nine individuals and seized four apparent vehicle-borne improvised explosives devices (VBIEDs) containing a total of over 1,100 kilograms of explosives.

Three of the VBIEDs were recovered by authorities on June 6. Of those, two vehicles contained 400 kilograms of explosives, while the third carried a 200-kilogram load, Malik said. On the same day, authorities advised that they were searching for a fourth VBIED, which appears to be the one they recovered June 9. According to Malik, it contained 180 kilograms of explosives.

The VBIED seizures follow the June 2 bombing of the Danish Embassy in Islamabad, which left eight people dead and many more wounded. In his press conference, Malik noted that three would-be suicide bombers were among those arrested. He also noted that the militants' attack plans were "fully mature" and that the group was close to launching attacks with the VBIEDs at the time they were arrested.

Tactically, Malik's assessment rings true, because militant groups do not make VBIEDs unless they intend to use them. Not only is the process expensive and labor-intensive, but it is far easier to cache and conceal bulk explosives than a fully assembled VBIED. Because VBIEDs are so easily discovered, one does not leave them sitting around; they are constructed and then quickly employed. Additionally, if an improvised explosive mixture is to be used as the main charge in the device, many of these mixtures are unstable and tend to degrade over time. They are best used fresh.

With these facts in mind, it is understandable that the U.S. Embassy in Islamabad issued a Warden Message after the June 6 seizure alerting U.S. citizens and advising them to maintain a low profile. The fact that the fourth device was seized on June 9 shows that the U.S. concern was justified. There are several militant actors in Pakistan, ranging from foreign groups like al Qaeda, which claimed credit for the Danish Embassy attack, to domestic actors such as Baitullah Mehsud's militant jihadist group, Tehrik-i-Taliban Pakistan (TTP).

It is not yet clear whether the seizure of the four VBIEDs resulted from the investigation into the Danish Embassy bombing (and is therefore tied to the perpetrators of that attack) or whether the devices belonged to another actor. There is, however, some indication of their provenance based on their size. There are also several other interesting points that can be gleaned by turning a protective intelligence lens on the facts at hand.

## Prior Warning

Like many other attacks, the strike against the Danish Embassy did not occur out of the blue. In early 2006, following the September 2005 publication of a series of cartoons satirizing the Prophet Mohammed, protests erupted in many parts of the Islamic world. While many Muslims protested the cartoons by boycotting Danish goods, others displayed their displeasure with violence. The Danish embassies in Beirut and Damascus were set on fire, and threats to Danes abounded in many countries. In August 2007, this outrage was inflamed again when a Swedish newspaper printed a controversial cartoon of the Prophet.

Things came to a boil again in early 2008 when Dutch parliamentarian Geert Wilders released a controversial film called Fitna, which harshly criticized Islam and used images of the Danish cartoons from 2005. Many Muslims were outraged by the film. Among those who reacted was Osama bin Laden, who in a March 19 statement threatened attacks against European countries. In fact, bin Laden even said the images were more provocative than killing Muslim civilians.

In the wake of these most recent threats, the Danes drew down their embassy staff in Islamabad. Recognizing that their embassy was not very secure, the Danes had many of their remaining Danish staff in Islamabad work out of hotels, which they believed were safer. The Dutch reacted similarly and actually moved their embassy to an Islamabad hotel in mid-April. In response to the threat, security was also ramped up around European embassies, including Denmark's, which continued to conduct many of its consular functions in its embassy building.

## The Target

The Danish Embassy is located in an upscale residential neighborhood outside of Islamabad's protected diplomatic enclave. In fact, it is located not far from Luna Caprese, a restaurant that was bombed on March 15, and the Marriott hotel, which was targeted by a suicide bomber in January 2007. While its location outside the diplomatic enclave made the facility more vulnerable to attack, perhaps the most critical factors in the embassy's vulnerability were its location in relation to the street and its construction.

The Danish Embassy is not only in a residential neighborhood — it also is a converted residence. As such, it was designed and built to shelter people in comfort and is not constructed of materials meant to withstand the force of an explosive attack. The vulnerability presented by this type of construction was compounded by the fact that the building was situated very close to the street. In a bombing attack, construction of the target is important, but the only thing that truly provides protection from the effects of a very large VBIED is standoff — keeping the bomb away from the protected building. With newer U.S. Embassy buildings (such as the one in Islamabad), the structures not only are built to withstand a blast or rocket attack but also are located a significant distance from the embassy compound perimeter. This positioning is intended to ensure protection from any blast.

In contrast, the Danish Embassy in Islamabad only had a few feet separating the perimeter wall from the building itself. Due to the building's construction and location, very little could have been done for its protection other than to close the street in front of it or, at the very least, to try and control the traffic. Many older embassies and consulates are situated in former residences or commercial buildings. As a result, in the realm of embassy security there is often tension between security officers, who want to shut down streets and provide standoff protection for their facilities, and the host government, which does not want further congestion in the typically crowded cities in which the facilities are often located. In the case of the Danish Embassy in Islamabad, which was not located on a main thoroughfare, it appears that the Pakistanis did establish roadblocks to control access to the area, which contained many other potential terrorist targets.

## The Attack

The vehicle used in the attack was a small, white Toyota or Suzuki. According to several media reports, the vehicle bore counterfeit Danish diplomatic license plates. The attack was caught on the embassy's closed-circuit television system, which, according to the Danish Security and Intelligence Service, reportedly shows the vehicle passing by the embassy, stopping and then reversing toward the building's vehicle gate before detonating.

The location of the seat of the blast (which marks where the vehicle was when it exploded) in relation to the embassy building and gate appears to confirm this report. In fact, the brunt of the force of the explosion missed the embassy building and instead destroyed a section of the embassy's perimeter wall adjacent to a parking lot. However, a U.N. building located across the street was not as lucky and experienced heavy damage from the explosion.

The fact that the bomber drove past his target would seem to indicate that he was poorly prepared for his mission — much to the good fortune of the Danes. Had he been able to detonate the device while on the street parallel to the embassy building, or had he been able to jump the curb and position the device directly against the perimeter wall, the damage to the embassy building would have been far worse, and the casualty count might have been higher.

The reports of the counterfeit Danish diplomatic license plates are also intriguing. While such plates likely helped the bomber get past the police checkpoints and onto the street where the embassy was located, the Danish Embassy is very small, and the guards there were undoubtedly familiar with all of the vehicles bearing Danish diplomatic tags. Therefore, it is highly unlikely that they would have allowed the vehicle to enter the embassy's perimeter, enabling the bomber to detonate the device in very close proximity to the building.

The timing of the attack is also very interesting. That it was conducted at 1 p.m. on a business day clearly indicates that the attackers intended to cause maximum casualties. Their efforts were not intended as a symbolic gesture, as might be suggested by, for example, an attack undertaken on a Saturday or at 3 a.m. While these particular aggressors were obviously after blood, their brutal intentions may have had limits. The embassy's visa section closes at noon, and it would appear that the attackers may have purposefully scheduled a later attack to minimize the casualties to Pakistani visa applicants. They also did not schedule the attack during the morning or afternoon rush, when there would be more people on the street.

While al Qaeda claimed the attack as a success, it killed mostly Pakistani Muslims and clearly did not create the type of "infidel" body count the planners would have hoped for. The only Danish citizen killed was born in Pakistan and held dual citizenship; the rest of the victims were also Pakistanis.

### Recovered VBIEDs

Whoever assembled the four recently seized VBIEDs devoted a significant amount of resources to their creation. From the sheer size of the devices alone, it can be clearly extrapolated that they were intended to create significant carnage and damage. One simply does not make a 400-kilogram VBIED for symbolism. A 5-kilogram device can be used to make a symbolic point — a 400-kilogram device is immensely destructive. The simultaneous employment of two such devices detonated in one city in conjunction with two other 200-kilogram devices could create a terrorist spectacular.

The size of the devices also speaks to the intended targets. A would-be terrorist does not need a 400-kilogram device to go after a soft target. While a 5-kilogram IED can easily take out a U.S. fast-food franchise, a larger VBIED is needed to damage hardened targets with robust construction. A 400-kilogram device detonated at the same spot as the June 2 attack would likely have leveled the Danish Embassy. By way of reference, such a device would be larger than those used by Hezbollah in Argentina to bomb the Israeli Embassy in 1992 or the Asociacion Mutual Israelita Argentina in 1994.

Some may contend that the Pakistani government has fabricated this threat and staged these arrests to create public reassurance while demonstrating its competence following the Danish Embassy bombing. Such a publicity stunt is unlikely, in our opinion, especially considering the extensive amount of explosives uncovered. In fact, by making this information public and showcasing the large amount of explosives that the attackers were able to obtain, the Pakistani government is illustrating just the opposite point. In effect, the Pakistanis have confirmed that an at-large organization inside their country possesses the ability to amass and employ nearly 1,200 kilograms of explosives. This news is not reassuring by any stretch of the imagination.

The recovered VBIEDs are evidence of both a serious and a costly effort. Even in Pakistan, 1,200 kilograms of explosives does not grow on trees. An organization willing to expend such energy, resources and time will not typically stop until it is destroyed or otherwise neutralized. It might make tactical changes based on lessons learned from failed operations, but it will continue to attack.

Pakistani militant groups are not shy about using explosives, but the majority of their devices — even suicide devices — are smaller. The size of the device and the fact that there were multiple devices involved would tend to point toward al Qaeda, which has a penchant for thinking big and has an operational history of conducting multiple, simultaneous attacks. In other words, these attacks appear to indicate that Pakistan's jihadist chickens are coming home to roost.

The bombing of the Danish Embassy and the recovery of the four large VBIEDs demonstrate that al Qaeda has the capability to mount serious attacks in Pakistan. The fact that the last four devices were discovered before they could be employed illustrates that the Pakistani government has some intelligence coverage regarding those capabilities.

At this point, however, it appears that al Qaeda, the TTP and other militants can operate with a large degree of freedom and that the Pakistani government does not have the ability to consistently prevent them from planning and launching attacks. From the intent and effort displayed by al Qaeda in the last several days, we anticipate more attempted attacks in Islamabad — including attacks on hard targets — in the foreseeable future.

This means that foreigners with interests in Pakistan would be well advised to heed the June 6 Warden Message, in spite of the recovery of the fourth VBIED. With militants' targeting plans likely to continue, it would also be prudent to ratchet up surveillance detection efforts at potential target sites.

---

## Protective Intelligence Assessment: The Islamabad Marriott Bombing
### Sept. 22, 2008

On Sept. 20, at approximately 8 p.m. local time, a large vehicle-borne improvised explosive device (VBIED) detonated in front of the Marriott Hotel in Islamabad, Pakistan. Pakistani sources report that the device contained approximately 2,000 pounds of explosives. Judging from photos of the blast crater (which was reportedly 24 to 30 feet deep and some 60 feet wide) as well as the size of the truck containing the device and the damage done to the hotel and surrounding neighborhood, that estimate is probably accurate.

The hotel was destroyed despite the fact that its extensive physical security measures operated as designed — they were overcome by the massive amount of explosive used. The success of the attack highlights the need for protective intelligence in addition to physical security measures.

The attack has been blamed on al Qaeda — which is a reasonable assumption, especially in light of the four large VBIEDs that were seized by Pakistani authorities in June and the VBIED attack on the Danish Embassy that was claimed by al Qaeda in a video showing the bomber's preparation. The four devices seized after the Danish Embassy attack contained a combined total of nearly 2,600 pounds of explosives. As we noted at the time those devices were seized, such large VBIEDs are very powerful, and are normally intended to be used in attacks on hard targets — targets with security that would prevent attacks by smaller devices.

There are unconfirmed reports that the Prime Minister House may have been the primary target for this attack but that the attackers found security too tight there and diverted to the Marriott instead. This is plausible. Secondary attack sites are commonly planned for VBIED attacks, and certainly either target would be high on al Qaeda's priority list. If this report is true, however, it is somewhat odd that the heightened security that allegedly prevented the truck from hitting the Prime Minister House did not notice the out-of-place truck and then act to interdict it.

It is important to note that the security measures in place at the Marriott did not fail. In fact, the security at his particular hotel was better than that employed at most hotels around the world, but it is very difficult to seal off completely a commercial building like a hotel. The physical security measures at the Marriott functioned as designed, and, in fact, managed to stop the truck at the hotel's exterior barricade. Had this attack employed a smaller device like the one deployed against the Danish Embassy, the damage to the hotel would have been much less. However, while the hotel's security measures — which prevented an attempt in January 2007 to attack the hotel by an operative wearing a suicide vest — were sufficient to protect against smaller devices, the attackers' use of a very large device overcame the standoff distance from the vehicle checkpoint to the hotel building itself, which was designed to be a luxury hotel and not a hardened facility such as a U.S. Embassy.

The explosive device in the truck did not detonate immediately; the vehicle stopped at the barrier, burst into flames and burned for several minutes (during which time the security personnel attempted to put out the flames with a fire extinguisher), and only then did it explode. Had security officers recognized that the truck contained a VBIED and begun to evacuate the hotel at that time, the number of casualties might have been reduced.

In the end, this was not a particularly sophisticated or elegant attack. Brute force — in the form of a huge explosive device — worked to overcome the security measures in place, and the damage done to the hotel appears to have been amplified by the inability to shut down the natural gas lines in the hotel. The resulting intense fires not only caused considerable additional damage to the structure but also greatly hampered rescue efforts.

With the security measures functioning as designed, the real failure was not in physical security but in protective intelligence. At the national level, Pakistani authorities failed to intercept the VBIED before it could be employed. On a tactical level, if hotel security or the authorities in Islamabad were using countersurveillance teams outside the hotel, they apparently failed to catch the pre-operational surveillance performed prior to the attack. Though in their defense, with such a high-profile target, one that has been hit by multiple attacks in the past, much of the targeting surveillance was undoubtedly conducted months ago and only a limited amount of surveillance would have been necessary to update plans and check current conditions at the target prior to launching the attack.

We wrote at the time the Pakistani authorities seized the four large VBIEDs in June that more attacks were likely, and some of that analysis bears quoting here because it remains applicable:

"At this point, however, it appears that al Qaeda, the Tehrik-i-Taliban Pakistan and other militants can operate with a large degree of freedom and that the Pakistani government does not have the ability to consistently prevent them from planning and launching attacks. From the intent and effort displayed by al Qaeda in the last several days, we anticipate more attempted attacks in Islamabad — including attacks on hard targets — in the foreseeable future.

"This means that foreigners with interests in Pakistan would be well advised to heed the June 6 Warden Message, in spite of the recovery of the fourth VBIED. With militants' targeting plans likely to continue, it would also be prudent to ratchet up surveillance detection efforts at potential target sites."

As we noted at the time, an organization that goes to the expense and effort to amass 2,600 pounds of explosives and fashion the material into very large and destructive VBIEDs typically will not stop attacking until it is destroyed or otherwise neutralized.

---

## Implications of the Manawan Attack
*April 2, 2009*

On March 31, Baitullah Mehsud, commander of the Tehrik-i-Taliban Pakistan (TTP), called The Associated Press and Reuters to claim responsibility for the March 29 attack against a Pakistani police academy in Manawan, which is near the eastern Pakistani city of Lahore and the Indian border. The attack had been previously claimed by a little-known group, Fedayeen al-Islam (FI), which also took responsibility for the bombing of the Marriott Hotel in Islamabad in September 2008. Mehsud has also released an Urdu-language audio message claiming responsibility for the Manawan attack as well as a failed March 23 attack on the headquarters of the Police Special Branch in Islamabad. Mehsud, who authorities claim was behind the March 3 attack on the Sri Lankan cricket team in Lahore, also warned that there would be additional attacks all across the country in retaliation for U.S. drone strikes in the Federally Administered Tribal Areas. He even threatened to launch attacks in Washington, D.C.

It is not clear at this point if the two claims of responsibility for the Manawan attack are indeed contradictory. If FI is an independent group, it is possible that it was working with Mehsud in the assault on the police academy. However, it is also quite possible that FI is either part of the larger TTP (which is an umbrella group with many factions) or perhaps just a nom de guerre used by the TTP to claim certain attacks. When a reporter asked about the FI claim, Mehsud refused to comment. Two things can be ascertained from this: that

Mehsud's organization has the ability to conduct these attacks, and that a major jihadist figure like Mehsud has no real need to claim the attacks of others to bolster his reputation. In fact, lying about such a thing would hurt his well-established reputation.

It is a good bet, therefore, that the TTP was in fact involved in the Manawan attack. The odds are even greater when one considers the intelligence reports from a few days prior to the attack: that Mehsud had dispatched a group of 22 operatives from his base in South Waziristan, through the town of Mianwali in southwestern Punjab, to conduct attacks in Lahore and Rawalpindi. Pakistani authorities were actively searching for those operatives when the attack occurred in Manawan.

While STRATFOR has already published a political assessment of the Manawan attack, we believe it might also be interesting to look at the incident from a protective intelligence standpoint and examine the tactical aspects of the operation in more detail.

### Sequence of Events

The attack on the police academy in Manawan happened at approximately 7:20 a.m. on March 29 as more than 800 unarmed police cadets were on the parade field for their regularly scheduled morning training. Witness reports suggest that there were 10 attackers who scaled the back wall of the academy and began to attack the cadets. Part of the attack team reportedly was dressed in police uniforms, while the rest reportedly wore shalwar kameez (traditional Pakistani dress). Several members of the team also wore suicide belts, and at least some of them carried large duffle bags (similar to those carried by the assailants in the November 2008 Mumbai attacks and the March 3 attack on the Sri Lankan cricket team in Lahore). The gunmen reportedly engaged the cadets with hand grenades and fire from assault rifles. As the gunmen raked the parade ground, many of the cadets reportedly fled the compound or barricaded themselves in various rooms inside the facility. Because the bulk of the people at the academy were cadets and not trained police, they were not issued firearms.

The armed guards at the academy were able to offer some resistance, but the attack team was able to make its way across the parade ground and into the barracks, where the attackers established defensive positions, apparently with the hope of initiating a prolonged hostage situation. Reports are conflicting as to how many hostages they were actually able to seize and control inside the barracks.

The Pakistani police and military responded aggressively to the attack. Within about 30 minutes, officers from the Elite Force — a highly trained branch of the Punjab Police responsible for counterterrorism — reportedly had surrounded the barracks building. By 9 a.m., paramilitary Pakistan Rangers and Pakistani army troops began to arrive. Many of the wounded cadets were evacuated from the parade ground using armored personnel carriers (APCs) to protect them from the attackers' fire. The attackers apparently attempted to use grenades to attack the APCs, but were met with heavy suppressive fire from the security forces. Pakistani forces also apparently used tear gas against the attackers, as well as the APCs and helicopter gunships. Eventually, the Elite Force went room to room to clear the barracks building of attackers. By 4 p.m., the siege had ended, with six of the attackers captured and four killed. (Three of the four reportedly killed themselves using suicide belts.) Despite initial reports of high casualties, it now appears that only eight police officers or cadets were killed in the attack, with more than 90 others wounded.

While armed assaults against paramilitary forces, convoys and other targets are common along the border with Afghanistan, this attack was only the second such attack in Lahore. Terrorist attacks in Pakistan have more commonly been committed by suicide bombers, and it appears that Mehsud's group may have embraced a change in tactics, perhaps influenced by the success of Mumbai. (However, as we will discuss below, this latest attack, like the attack on the cricket team, was far from a spectacular success.)

First, it must be recognized that jihadist attacks on police recruits are not uncommon. We have seen attacks on police training and

# MANAWAN, PAKISTAN

recruiting centers in Iraq and Afghanistan, among other countries, and we have also seen them before in Pakistan. On July 15, 2007, a suicide bomber attacked a police recruitment center in Dera Ismail Khan, killing 26 people and wounding 35. The victims were at the center to take medical and written tests for entering the police force.

A training center like the one in Manawan provides an unusually large concentration of targets. The more than 800 cadets at the academy were a far larger group of police than is normally found in the police stations scattered throughout the country. The training center was also a far softer target than a traditional police station, where all the officers are armed. From media reports, it appears that there were only seven armed guards on duty at the academy at the time of the attack. The instructors allegedly were armed only with lathis (long canes commonly used by police in India and Pakistan). The academy's rigid training schedule also provided a highly predictable target, as the attackers knew the cadets would be on the parade field from 7 a.m. to 8 a.m. every day.

With so many potential targets on the parade field and in the barracks, and with so many attackers, it is amazing that there were only eight people killed in this attack (one-fourth the death toll of the April 2007 Virginia Tech shooting). This is an indication that the Manawan attackers were not nearly as well trained in marksmanship as the assault team that conducted the November Mumbai attacks, in which 10 gunmen killed 173 people. The 10 heavily armed Manawan assailants did not even succeed in killing one victim each in a situation akin to shooting fish in a barrel.

From a military standpoint, such a formation of massed people in the open would have been far more effectively targeted using mortars and crew-served machine guns, so it can also be argued that the attack was poorly planned and the attackers improperly equipped to inflict maximum casualties. Even so, it is quite amazing to us that attackers armed with assault rifles and grenades did not kill one victim apiece.

Of course, one thing that helped contain the carnage was the response of Pakistani security personnel and their efforts to evacuate the wounded under fire. While not exactly practicing what are known in the United States as "active shooter procedures," the Elite Force officers did quickly engage the attackers and pin them down until more firepower could be brought to bear. The Elite Force also did a fairly efficient job of clearing the barracks of attackers. The Pakistani response ensured that the incident did not drag on like the Mumbai attacks did. The Elite Force went in hard and fast, and seemingly with little regard for the hostages being held, yet their decisive action proved to be very effective, and the result was that a minimum number of hostages were killed.

There were some significant differences from the situation in Mumbai. First, there was only one crime scene to deal with, and the Pakistani authorities could focus all their attention and resources there. Second, the barracks building was far smaller and simpler than the hotels occupied in the Mumbai attacks. Third, Manawan is far smaller and more isolated than Mumbai, and it is easier to pin the attackers down in a city of that size than in a larger, more densely populated city such as Mumbai. Finally, there were no foreign citizens involved in the hostage situation, so the Pakistani authorities did not have to worry about international sensibilities or killing a foreign citizen with friendly fire. They were able to act aggressively and not worry about distractions — or the media circus that Mumbai became.

## The Future

Perhaps the most important thing to watch going forward will be the response of the Pakistani people to these attacks. In his claim of responsibility, Mehsud said the Manawan attack was in direct response to the expanding U.S. unmanned aerial vehicle (UAV) campaign in Pakistan. Mehsud threatened that there would be more militant attacks in Pakistan and the United States if the UAV attacks did not stop. Clearly, Mehsud is feeling the heat from these attacks, and although he claims he is ready to be martyred, his bravado is belied by the fact that he is taking such extraordinary measures to try to halt the UAV campaign. He obviously fears the UAV strikes, not only for what they can do to him but also for what they can do to degrade his organization.

When the Elite Force completed the clearing of the barracks, several officers came out on the roof of the building, shouted "God is great" and fired celebratory shots into the air (something that is anathema to Western police and military forces). Many of the people gathered outside the academy joined in the shouting and loudly cheered the Elite Force. This sentiment was widely echoed in the Pakistani media.

Although the Manawan attack was intended to demoralize Pakistani security forces, it may have just the opposite effect. The bravery and dedication exhibited by the Pakistani police and soldiers who responded to the attack may instead serve to steel their will and instill professional pride. Mehsud's recent threats, along with the militant attacks, may also work to alienate him from people who had been supportive of — or at least ambivalent toward — him and the jihadists.

Up until 2003, the Saudi public, and many in the government, pretty much turned a blind eye to the actions of jihadists in Saudi Arabia as long as the jihadists were concentrating their attacks on targets outside the kingdom. But when the jihadists declared war on the Saudi royal family and began to conduct attacks against targets inside the kingdom that resulted in the deaths of ordinary Saudis, the tide of public opinion turned against them and the Saudi government reacted aggressively, smashing the jihadists. Similarly, it was the brutality of al Qaeda in Iraq that helped turn many Iraqi Sunnis against the jihadists there. Indeed, an insurgency cannot survive long without the support of the people. In the case of Pakistan, that also goes for the support of Inter-Services Intelligence and the army. The TTP, al Qaeda and their Kashmiri militant allies simply cannot sustain themselves without at least the tacit support of Pakistan's intelligence apparatus and army. If these two powerful establishments ever turn against them, the groups will be in serious peril.

Pakistan has long been able to control the TTP and al Qaeda more than it has. The country has simply lacked the will, for a host of reasons. It will be interesting to watch and see if Mehsud's campaign serves to give the Pakistani people, and the authorities, the will they need to finally take more serious steps to tackle the jihadist problem. Having long battled deep currents of jihadist thought within the country, the Pakistani government continues to face serious challenges. But if the tide of public support begins to turn against the jihadists, those challenges will become far more manageable.

---

# Security at Places of Worship:
## More than a Matter of Faith
### *June 17, 2009*

In recent months, several high-profile incidents have raised awareness of the threat posed by individuals and small groups operating under the principles of leaderless resistance. These incidents have included lone wolf attacks against a doctor who performed abortions in Kansas, an armed forces recruitment center in Arkansas and the U.S. Holocaust Memorial Museum in Washington, D.C. Additionally, a grassroots jihadist cell was arrested for attempting to bomb Jewish targets in the Bronx and planning to shoot down a military aircraft at an Air National Guard base in Newburgh, N.Y.

In addition to pointing out the threat posed by grassroots cells and lone wolf operatives, another common factor in all of these incidents is the threat of violence to houses of worship. The cell arrested in New York left what they thought to be active improvised explosive devices outside the Riverdale Temple and the Riverdale Jewish Community Center. Dr. George Tiller was shot and killed in the lobby of the Reformation Lutheran Church in Wichita. Although Abdulhakim Mujahid Muhammad conducted his attack against a Little Rock recruiting center, he had conducted pre-operational surveillance and research on targets that included Jewish organizations and a Baptist church in places as far away as Atlanta and Philadelphia. And while

James von Brunn attacked the Holocaust Museum, he had a list of other potential targets in his vehicle that included the National Cathedral.

In light of this common thread, it might be instructive to take a more detailed look at the issue of providing security for places of worship.

## Awareness: The First Step

Until there is awareness of the threat, little can be done to counter it. In many parts of the world, such as Iraq, India and Pakistan, attacks against places of worship occur fairly frequently. It is not difficult for religious leaders and members of their congregations in such places to be acutely aware of the dangers facing them and to have measures already in place to deal with those perils. This is not always the case in the United States, however, where many people tend to have an "it can't happen here" mindset, believing that violence in or directed against places of worship is something that happens only to other people elsewhere.

This mindset is particularly pervasive among predominantly white American Protestant and Roman Catholic congregations. Jews, Mormons, Muslims and black Christians, and others who have been targeted by violence in the past, tend to be far more aware of the threat and are far more likely to have security plans and measures in place to counter it. The Jewish community has very well-developed and professional organizations such as the Secure Community Network (SCN) and the Anti-Defamation League that are dedicated to monitoring threats and providing education about the threats and advice regarding security. The Council on American-Islamic Relations has taken on a similar role for the Muslim community and has produced a "Muslim community safety kit" for local mosques. The Church of Jesus Christ of Latter-day Saints (LDS) also has a very organized and well-connected security department that provides information and security advice and assistance to LDS congregations worldwide.

There are no functional equivalents to the SCN or the LDS security department in the larger Catholic, evangelical Protestant and mainline Protestant communities, though there are some organizations such as the recently established Christian Security Network that have been attempting to fill the void.

Following an incident, awareness of the threat seems to rise for a time, and some houses of worship will put some security measures in place, but for the most part such incidents are seen as events that take place elsewhere, and the security measures are abandoned after a short time.

Permanent security measures are usually not put in place until there has been an incident of some sort at a specific house of worship, and while the triggering incident is sometimes something that merely provides a good scare, other times it is a violent action that results in tragedy. Even when no one is hurt in the incident, the emotional damage caused to a community by an act of vandalism or arson at a house of worship can be devastating.

It is important to note here that not all threats to places of worship will emanate from external actors. In the midst of any given religious congregation, there are, by percentages, people suffering from serious mental illnesses and people engaged in bitter child-custody disputes, domestic violence situations and messy divorces. Internal disputes in the congregation can also lead to feuds and violence. Any of these situations can (and have) led to acts of violence inside houses of worship.

### Security Means More than Alarms and Locks

An effective security program is more than just having physical security measures in place. Like any man-made constructs, physical security measures — closed-circuit television (CCTV), alarms, cipher locks and so forth — have finite utility. They serve a valuable purpose in institutional security programs, but an effective security program cannot be limited to these things. Devices cannot think or evaluate. They are static and can be observed, learned and even fooled.

Also, because some systems frequently produce false alarms, warnings in real danger situations may be brushed aside. Given these short-comings, it is quite possible for anyone planning an act of violence to map out, quantify and then defeat or bypass physical security devices. However, elaborate planning is not always necessary. Consider the common scenario of a heavy metal door with very good locks that is propped open with a trash can or a door wedge. In such a scenario, an otherwise "secure" door is defeated by an internal security lapse.

However, even in situations where there is a high degree of threat awareness, there is a tendency to place too much trust in physical security measures, which can become a kind of crutch — and, ironically, an obstacle to effective security.

In fact, to be effective, physical security devices always require human interaction. An alarm is useless if no one responds to it, or if it is not turned on; a lock is ineffective if it is not engaged. CCTV cameras are used extensively in corporate office buildings and some houses of worship, but any competent security manager will tell you that, in reality, they are far more useful in terms of investigating a theft or act of violence after the fact than in preventing one (although physical security devices can sometimes cause an attacker to divert to an easier target).

No matter what kinds of physical security measures may be in place at a facility, they are far less likely to be effective if a potential assailant feels free to conduct surveillance, and is free to observe and map those physical security measures. The more at ease someone feels as they set about identifying and quantifying the physical security systems and procedures in place, the higher the odds they will find ways to beat the system.

A truly "hard" target is one that couples physical security measures with an aggressive, alert attitude and sense of awareness. An effective security program is proactive — focused on recognizing potential threats before they present themselves as active threats. We refer to this process of proactively looking for threats as protective intelligence.

The human interaction required to make physical security measures effective, and to transform a security program into a proactive protective intelligence program, can come in the form of designated security personnel. In fact, many large houses of worship do utilize off-duty police officers, private security guards, volunteer security guards or even a dedicated security staff to provide this coverage. In smaller congregations, security personnel can be members of the congregation who have been provided some level of training.

However, even in cases where there are specially designated security personnel, such officers have only so many eyes and can only be in a limited number of places at any one time. Thus, proactive security programs should also work to foster a broad sense of security awareness among the members of the congregation and community, and use them as additional resources.

Unfortunately, in many cases, there is often a sense in the religious community that security is bad for the image of a particular institution, or that it will somehow scare people away from houses of worship. Because of this, security measures, if employed, are often hidden or concealed from the congregation. In such cases, security managers are deprived of many sets of eyes and ears. Certainly, there may be certain facets of a security plan that not everyone in the congregation needs to know about, but in general, an educated and aware congregation and community can be a very valuable security asset.

## Training

In order for a congregation to maintain a sense of heightened awareness it must learn how to effectively do that. This training should not leave people scared or paranoid — just more observant. People need to be trained to look for individuals who are out of place, which can be somewhat counterintuitive. By nature, houses of worship are open to outsiders and seek to welcome strangers. They frequently have a steady turnover of new faces. This causes many to believe that, in houses of worship, there is a natural antagonism between security and openness, but this does not have to be the case. A house of worship can have both a steady stream of visitors and good security, especially if that security is based upon situational awareness.

At its heart, situational awareness is about studying people, and such scrutiny will allow an observer to pick up on demeanor mistakes that might indicate someone is conducting surveillance. Practicing awareness and paying attention to the people approaching or inside a house of worship can also open up a whole new world of ministry opportunities, as people "tune in" to others and begin to perceive things they would otherwise miss if they were self-absorbed or simply not paying attention. In other words, practicing situational awareness provides an excellent opportunity for the members of a congregation to focus on the needs and burdens of other people.

It is important to remember that every attack cycle follows the same general steps. All criminals — whether they are stalkers, thieves, lone wolves or terrorist groups — engage in surveillance (sometimes called "casing," in the criminal lexicon). Perhaps the most crucial point to be made about surveillance is that it is the phase when someone with hostile intentions is most apt to be detected — and the point in the attack cycle when potential violence can be most easily disrupted or prevented.

The second most critical point to emphasize about surveillance is that most criminals are not that good at it. They often have terrible surveillance tradecraft and are frequently very obvious. Most often, the only reason they succeed in conducting surveillance without being detected is because nobody is looking for them. Because of this, even ordinary people, if properly instructed, can note surveillance activity.

It is also critically important to teach people — including security personnel and members of the congregation — what to do if they see something suspicious and whom to call to report it. Unfortunately, a lot of critical intelligence is missed because it is not reported in a timely manner — or not reported at all — mainly because untrained people have a habit of not trusting their judgment and dismissing unusual activity. People need to be encouraged to report what they see.

Additionally, people who have been threatened, are undergoing nasty child-custody disputes or have active restraining orders protecting them against potentially violent people need to be encouraged to report unusual activity to their appropriate points of contact.

As part of their security training, houses of worship should also instruct their staff and congregation members on procedures to follow if a shooter enters the building and creates what is called an active-shooter situation. These "shooter" drills should be practiced regularly — just like fire, tornado or earthquake drills. The teachers of children's classes and nursery workers must also be trained in how to react.

## Liaison

One of the things the SCN and ADL do very well is foster security liaison among Jewish congregations within a community and between those congregations and local, state and federal law enforcement organizations. This is something that houses of worship from other faiths should attempt to duplicate as part of their security plans.

While having a local cop in a congregation is a benefit, contacting the local police department should be the first step. It is very important to establish this contact before there is a crisis in order to help expedite any law enforcement response. Some police departments even have dedicated community liaison officers, who are good points of initial contact. There are other specific points of contact that should also be cultivated within the local department, such as the SWAT team and the bomb squad.

Local SWAT teams often appreciate the chance to do a walk-through of a house of worship so that they can learn the layout of the building in case they are ever called to respond to an emergency there. They also like the opportunity to use different and challenging buildings for training exercises (something that can be conducted discreetly after hours). Congregations with gyms and weight rooms will often open them up for local police officers to exercise in, and some congregations will also offer police officers a cup of coffee and a desk where they can sit and type their reports during evening hours.

But the local police department is not the only agency with which liaison should be established. Depending on the location of the house of worship, the state police, state intelligence fusion center or local joint terrorism task force should also be contacted. By working through state and federal channels, houses of worship in specific locations may even be eligible for grants to help underwrite security through programs such as the Department of Homeland Security's Urban Areas Security Initiative Nonprofit Security Grant Program.

The world is a dangerous place and attacks against houses of worship will continue to occur. But there are proactive security measures that can be taken to identify attackers before they strike and help prevent attacks from happening or mitigate their effects when they do.

---

## Examining the Jakarta Attacks: Trends and Challenges
### *July 22, 2009*

On the morning of July 17, a guest at the JW Marriott hotel in Jakarta came down to the lobby and began walking toward the lounge with his roll-aboard suitcase in tow and a backpack slung across his chest. Sensing something odd about the fellow, alert security officers approached him and asked him if he required assistance. The guest responded that he needed to deliver the backpack to his boss and proceeded to the lounge, accompanied by one of the security guards. Shortly after entering the lounge, the guest activated the improvised explosive device (IED) contained in the backpack, killing himself and five others. Minutes later, an accomplice detonated a second IED in a restaurant at the adjacent Ritz-Carlton hotel, killing himself and two other victims, bringing the death toll from the operation to nine — including six foreigners.

The twin bombings in Jakarta underscore two tactical trends that STRATFOR has been following for several years now, namely, the targeting of hotels in terrorist attacks and the use of smaller suicide devices to circumvent physical security measures. The Jakarta attacks also highlight the challenges associated with protecting soft targets such as hotels against such attacks.

### The Iconic Target

During the 1970s the iconic terrorist target became the international airliner. But as airline security increased in response to terrorist incidents, it became more difficult to hijack or bomb aircraft, and this difficulty resulted in a shift in targeting. By the mid-1980s, while there were still some incidents involving aircraft, the iconic terrorist target had become the embassy. But attacks against embassies have also provoked a security response, resulting in embassy security programs that have produced things like the American "Inman buildings," which some have labeled "fortress America" buildings due to their foreboding presence and their robust construction designed to withstand rocket and large IED attacks. Due to these changes, it became far more difficult to attack embassies, many of which have become, for the most part in our post-9/11 world, hard targets. (This is certainly not universal, and there are still vulnerable embassies in many places. In fact, some countries locate their embassies inside commercial office buildings or hotels.)

Overall, however, this trend of making embassies hard targets has caused yet another shift in the terrorist paradigm. As STRATFOR has noted since 2004, hotels have become the iconic terrorist target of the post-9/11 era. Indeed, by striking an international hotel in a capital city, militants can make the same type of statement against Western imperialism and decadence that they can make by striking an embassy. Hotels are often full of Western businessmen, diplomats and intelligence officers, providing militants with a target-rich environment where they can kill Westerners and gain international media attention without having to penetrate the extreme security of a modern embassy.

Our 2004 observation about the trend toward attacking hotels has been borne out since that time by attacks against hotels in several parts of the world, including Pakistan, Afghanistan, Iraq, Jordan, India and Egypt. In addition to attacks against single hotels, in the attacks in Mumbai, Amman, Sharm el-Sheikh — and now Jakarta — militants staged coordinated attacks in which they hit more than one hotel.

Hotels have taken measures to improve security, and hotel security overall is better today than it was in 2004. In fact, security measures in place at several hotels, such as the Marriott in Islamabad, have saved lives on more than one occasion. However, due to the very nature of hotels, they remain vulnerable to attacks.

Unlike an embassy, a hotel is a commercial venture and is intended to make money. In order to make money, the hotel needs to maintain a steady flow of customers who stay in its rooms; visitors who eat at its restaurants, drink at its bars and rent its banquet and conference facilities; and merchants who rent out its shop space. On any given day a large five-star hotel can have hundreds of guests staying there, hundreds of other visitors attending conferences or dinner events and scores of other people eating in the restaurants, using the health club or shopping at the luxury stores commonly found inside such hotels. Such amenities are often difficult to find outside of such hotels in cities like Peshawar or Kabul, and therefore these hotels also become gathering places for foreign businessmen, diplomats and journalists as well as wealthy natives. It is fairly easy for a militant operative to conduct surveillance of the inside of a hotel by posing as a restaurant patron or by shopping in its stores.

Of course, the staff required to run such a huge facility can also number in the hundreds, with clerks, cooks, housekeepers, waiters, bellboys, busboys, valets, florists, gardeners, maintenance men, security personnel, etc. These hotels are like little cities with activities that run 24 hours a day, with people, luggage, food and goods coming and going at all hours. There are emerging reports that one of the suicide

# THE JAKARTA BOMBINGS

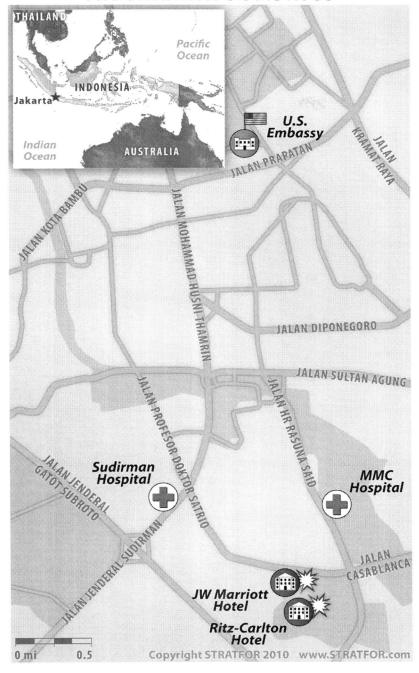

THAILAND

Pacific
Ocean

INDONESIA

Jakarta

Indian
Ocean

AUSTRALIA

U.S.
Embassy

JALAN PRAPATAN

JALAN KRAMAT RAYA

JALAN KOTA BAMBU

JALAN MOHAMMAD HUSNI THAMRIN

JALAN DIPONEGORO

JALAN SULTAN AGUNG

JALAN PROFESOR DOKTOR SATRIO

JALAN HR RASUNA SAID

JALAN JENDERAL GATOT SUBROTO

Sudirman
Hospital

MMC
Hospital

JALAN JENDERAL SUDIRMAN

JALAN CASABLANCA

JW Marriott
Hotel

Ritz-Carlton
Hotel

0 mi          0.5

bombers in the Jakarta attack was a florist at one of the hotels, and it is possible that he used his position to smuggle IED components into the facility among floral supplies. If true, the long-term place-ment of militant operatives within the hotel staff will pose daunting challenges to corporate security directors. Such an inside placement could also explain how the cell responsible for the attack was able to conduct the detailed surveillance required for the operation without being detected.

Quite simply, it is extremely expensive to provide a hotel with the same level of physical security afforded to an embassy. Land to pro-vide standoff distance is very expensive in many capital cities and heavy reinforced-concrete construction to withstand attacks costs far more than regular commercial construction. Such costs must be weighed against the corporate bottom line.

Moreover, security procedures at an embassy such as screening 100 percent of the visitors and their belongings are deemed far too intru-sive by many hotel managers, and there is a constant tension between hotel security managers and hotel guest-relations managers over how much security is required in a particular hotel in a specific city. In fact, this debate over security is very similar to the tension that exists between diplomats and security personnel at the U.S. Department of State. And the longer the period between successful attacks (there had not been a successful terrorist attack in Jakarta since September 2004 and in Indonesia since October 2005), the harder it is to jus-tify the added expense — and inconvenience — of security measures at hotels. (Of course, in very dangerous places such as Baghdad, Islamabad and Kabul heavy security is far easier to justify, and some hotels in such locations have been heavily fortified following attacks on other hotels in those cities.)

In many places, hotel guests are subjected to less security scru-tiny than visitors to the hotel, as the hotel staff seeks to make them feel welcomed, and it is not surprising that militants in places like Mumbai (and perhaps Jakarta) have been able to smuggle weapons and IED components into a hotel concealed inside their luggage. We have received a report from a credible source indicating that one of the

Jakarta attackers had indeed been checked into the JW Marriott hotel. The source says the attacker, posing as a guest, was an Indonesian but was likely from a remote area because he did not appear to be familiar with how to use modern conveniences such as the room's Western-style toilet. That the attackers were Indonesians supports the theory that the attack was conducted by the Southeast Asian group Jemaah Islamiyah (JI) or a JI splinter group. JI has conducted (or is a suspect in) every high-profile terror attack in Indonesia in recent years.

Sources advise us that significant similarities exist between the unexploded device discovered in the attacker's hotel room in the JW Marriott and known JI explosive devices used in past attacks and recovered in police raids. This is another strong indication JI was involved.

One other important lesson that travelers should take from this string of hotel attacks is that, while they should pay attention to the level of security provided at hotels, and stay at hotels with better security, they should not rely exclusively on hotel security to keep them safe. There are some simple personal security measures that should also be taken to help mitigate the risk of staying at a hotel.

## Size is Not Everything

As STRATFOR has noted since 2005, the counterterrorism tactic of erecting barricades around particularly vulnerable targets — including government buildings such as embassies and softer targets such as hotels — has forced militants to rethink their attack strategies and adapt. Instead of building bigger and bigger bombs that could possibly penetrate more secure areas, operational planners are instead thinking small — and mobile. In fact, it was the October 2005 triple-bomb attacks against restaurants in Bali, Indonesia, by JI, and the November 2005 triple suicide-bombing attacks against three Western hotels in Amman, Jordan, that really focused our attention on this trend.

Like the July 7, 2005, London bombings, these two attacks in Jakarta and Amman used smaller-scale explosive devices to bypass security and target areas where people congregate. Such attacks demonstrated an evolution in militant tactics away from large and bulky explosives and toward smaller, more portable devices that can be used in a wider variety of situations. Flexibility provides many options, and in the case of the operative who attacked the JW Marriott on July 17, it appears that he was able to approach a meeting of foreign businessmen being held in the lobby lounge and attack them as a target of opportunity. A vehicle-borne IED (VBIED) detonated in front of the hotel would not likely have been able to target such a group so selectively on the fly.

Of course, this trend does not mean that large VBIEDs will never again be employed any more than the trend to attack hotels means aircraft and embassies will never be attacked. Rather, our intent here is to point out that, as security has been increased around targets, militants have adapted to those measures and have changed their tactics accordingly.

At first glance, it would seem logical that the shift from large VBIEDs would cause casualty counts to drop, but in the case of JI attacks in Indonesia, the shift to smaller devices has, in fact, caused higher casualty counts. The August 2003 attack against the JW Marriott in Jakarta used a VBIED and left 12 people dead. Likewise, the September 2004 attack against the Australian embassy in Jakarta used a VBIED and killed 10 people. The use of three smaller IEDs in the 2005 Bali attacks killed 23, more than JI's 2003 and 2004 VBIED attacks combined. Additionally, the 2005 attacks killed five foreigners as opposed to only one in the 2003 attack and none in the 2004 attacks. The operatives behind the July 17 attacks surpassed the 2005 Bali attacks by managing to kill six foreigners.

The reason that smaller is proving to be more effective at killing foreigners is that the rule for explosives is much like real estate — the three most important factors are location, location and location. Though a larger quantity of explosives will create a larger explosion, the impact of an explosion is determined solely by placement. If a bomber can carry a smaller explosive into the center of a heavily packed crowd — such as a wedding reception or hotel lobby — it will cause more damage than a larger device detonated farther away from its intended target. These smaller devices can also be used to target a specific person, as seen in the December 2007 assassination of former Pakistani Prime Minister Benazir Bhutto.

A person carrying explosives in a bag or concealed under clothing is much more fluid and can maneuver into the best possible position before detonating. In essence, a suicide bomber is a very sophisticated form of "smart" munition that can work its way through gaps in security and successfully seek its target. This type of guidance appears to have worked very effectively in the July 17 Jakarta attacks. As noted above, of the seven victims in this attack (the nine total deaths included the bombers), six were foreigners. JI has been criticized by the Islamist community in Indonesia for killing innocent bystanders (and Muslims), and such targeted attacks will help mute such criticism.

In addition to being more efficient, smaller IEDs also are cheaper to make. In an environment where explosive material is difficult to obtain, it is far easier to assemble the material for two or three small devices than the hundreds of pounds required for a large VBIED. An attack like the July 17 Jakarta attack could have been conducted at a very low cost, probably not more than a few thousand dollars. The three devices employed in that attack (as noted above, there was a third device left in the hotel room that did not explode) likely did not require much more than 60 pounds of explosive material.

This economical approach to terrorism is a distinct advantage for a militant group like Noordin Mohammad Top's faction of JI, Tanzim Qaedat al-Jihad. Due to the Indonesian government's crackdown on JI and its factions, the Indonesian militants simply do not have the external funding and freedom of action they enjoyed prior to the October 2002 Bali attack. This means that, at the present time, it would be very difficult for JI to purchase or otherwise procure the hundreds of pounds of explosive material required for a large VBIED — coming up with 60 pounds is far easier.

Even though JI is fragmented and its abilities have been degraded since the 2002 Bali attack, a cell like the one headed by Top certainly maintains the ability and the expertise to conduct low-cost, carefully targeted attacks like the July 17 Jakarta bombings. Such attacks are easily sustainable, and the only real limiter on the group's ability to conduct similar attacks in the future is finding attackers willing to kill themselves in the process. Perhaps a more significant limiter on their operational tempo will be the law enforcement response to the attack, which could force the cell to go underground until the heat is off. It might also be difficult to move operatives and IEDs from safe houses to targets when there is more scrutiny of potential JI militants.

Increased security at potential targets could also cause the cell to wait until complacency sets in before attacking a less wary — and softer — target. Of course, the group's operational ability will also be affected should the Indonesian government capture or kill key operatives like Top and his lieutenants.

From the standpoint of security, the challenges of balancing security with guest comfort and customer service at large hotels will continue to be a vexing problem, though certainly it would not be surprising to see an increase in the use of magnetometers and X-ray machines to screen guests and visitors at vulnerable facilities. This may also include such measures as random bomb-dog searches and sweeps in areas where dogs are not a cultural taboo. Additionally, in light of the threat of suicide bombers using smaller devices or posing as guests, or even placing operatives on the hotel staff, much more effort will be made to implement proactive security measures such as protective intelligence and countersurveillance, which focus more on identifying potential attackers than on his or her weapons.

Hotel staff members also need to be taught that security is not just the role of the designated security department. Security officers are not omnipresent; they require other people on the hotel staff who have interactions with the guests and visitors to be their eyes and ears and to alert them to individuals who have made it through security and into the hotel and appear to be potential threats. Of course, the traveling public also has a responsibility not only to look out for their own personal security but to maintain a heightened state of situational awareness and notify hotel security of any unusual activity.

# Convergence: The Challenge of Aviation Security
### *Sept. 16, 2009*

On Sept. 13, As-Sahab media released an audio statement purportedly made by Osama bin Laden that was intended to address the American people on the anniversary of the 9/11 attacks. In the message, the voice alleged to be that of bin Laden said the reason for the 9/11 attacks was U.S. support for Israel. He also said that if the American people wanted to free themselves from "fear and intellectual terrorism," the United States must cut its support for Israel. If the United States continues to support Israel, the voice warned, al Qaeda would continue its war against the United States "on all possible fronts" — a not so subtle threat of additional terrorist attacks.

Elsewhere on Sept. 14, a judge at Woolwich Crown Court in the United Kingdom sentenced four men to lengthy prison sentences for their involvement in the disrupted 2006 plot to destroy multiple aircraft over the Atlantic using liquid explosives. The man authorities claimed was the leader of the cell, Abdulla Ahmed Ali, was sentenced to serve at least 40 years. The cell's apparent logistics man, Assad Sarwar, was sentenced to at least 36 years. Cell member Tanvir Hussain was given a sentence of at least 32 years and cell member Umar Islam was sentenced to a minimum of 22 years in prison.

The convergence of these two events (along with the recent release of convicted Pan Am 103 bomber Abdel Basset Ali al-Megrahi and the amateurish Sept. 9 hijacking incident in Mexico using a hoax improvised explosive device [IED]) has drawn our focus back to the topic of aviation security — in particular, IED attacks against aircraft. As we weave the strands of these independent events together, they remind us not only that attacks against aircraft are dramatic, generate a lot of publicity and can cause very high body counts (9/11), but also that such attacks can be conducted simply and quite inexpensively with an eye toward avoiding preventative security measures (the 2006 liquid-explosives plot).

Additionally, while the 9/11 anniversary reminds us that some jihadist groups have demonstrated a fixation on attacking aviation targets — especially those militants influenced by the operational philosophies of Khalid Sheikh Mohammed (KSM) — the convictions in the 2006 plot highlight the fact that the fixation on aviation targets lives on even after the 2003 arrest of KSM.

In response to this persistent threat, aviation security has changed dramatically in the post-9/11 era, and great effort has been undertaken at great expense to make attacks against passenger aircraft more difficult. Airline attacks are harder to conduct now than in the past, and while many militants have shifted their focus onto easier targets like subways or hotels, there are still some jihadists who remain fixated on the aviation target, and we will undoubtedly see more attempts against passenger aircraft in spite of the restrictions on the quantities of liquids that can be taken aboard aircraft and the now mandatory shoe inspections.

Quite simply, militants will seek alternate ways to smuggle components for IEDs aboard aircraft, and this is where another thread comes in — that of the Aug. 28 assassination attempt against Saudi Deputy Interior Minister Prince Mohammed bin Nayef. The tactical innovation employed in this attack highlights the vulnerabilities that still exist in airline security.

### Shifts

The airline security paradigm changed on 9/11. In spite of the recent statement by al Qaeda leader Mustafa Abu al-Yazid that al Qaeda retains the ability to conduct 9/11-style attacks, his boast simply does not ring true. After the 9/11 attacks there is no way a captain and crew (or a group of passengers for that matter) are going to relinquish control of an aircraft to hijackers armed with box cutters — or even a handgun or IED. A commercial airliner will never again be commandeered from the cockpit and flown into a building — especially in the United States.

Because of the shift in mindset and improvements in airline security, the militants have been forced to alter their operational framework. In effect they have returned to the pre-9/11 operational concept of taking down an aircraft with an IED rather than utilizing an aircraft as a human-guided missile. This return was first demonstrated by the December 2001 attempt by Richard Reid to destroy American Airlines Flight 63 over the Atlantic with a shoe bomb and later by the thwarted 2006 liquid-explosives plot. The operational concept in place now is clearly to destroy rather than commandeer. Both the Reid plot and the 2006 liquid-bomb plot show links back to the operational philosophy evidenced by Operation Bojinka in the mid-1990s, which was a plot to destroy multiple aircraft in flight over the Pacific Ocean.

The return to Bojinka principles is significant because it represents not only an IED attack against an aircraft but also a specific method of attack: a camouflaged, modular IED that the bomber smuggles onto an aircraft in pieces and then assembles once he or she is aboard and well past security. The original Bojinka plot used baby dolls to smuggle the main explosive charge of nitrocellulose aboard the aircraft. Once on the plane, the main charge was primed with an improvised detonator that was concealed inside a carry-on bag and then hooked into a power source and a timer (which was disguised as a wrist watch). The baby-doll device was successfully smuggled past security in a test run in December 1994 and was detonated aboard Philippine Air Flight 434.

The main charge in the baby-doll devices, however, proved insufficient to bring down the aircraft, so the plan was amended to add a supplemental charge of liquid triacetone triperoxide (or TATP, aptly referred to as "Mother of Satan"), which was to be concealed in a bottle of contact lens solution. The plot unraveled when the bombmaker, Abdel Basit (who is frequently referred to by one of his alias names, Ramzi Yousef) accidentally started his apartment on fire while brewing the TATP.

## The Twist

The 2006 liquid-bomb plot borrowed the elements of using liquid explosives and disguised individual components and attacking multiple aircraft at the same time from Bojinka. The 2006 plotters sought to smuggle their liquid explosives aboard using drink bottles instead of contact lens solution containers and planned to use different types of initiators. The biggest difference between Bojinka and more recent plots is that the Bojinka operatives were to smuggle the components aboard the aircraft, assemble the IEDs inside the lavatory and then leave the completed devices hidden aboard multi-leg flights while the operatives got off the aircraft at an intermediate stop. The more recent iterations of the jihadist airplane-attack concept, including Richard Reid's attempted shoe bombing and the 2006 liquid-bomb plot, planned to use suicide bombers to detonate the devices mid-flight. The successful August 2004 twin aircraft bombings in Russia by Chechen militants also utilized suicide bombers.

The shift to suicide operatives is not only a reaction to increased security but also the result of an evolution in ideology — suicide bombings have become more widely embraced by jihadist militants than they were in the early 1990s. As a result, the jihadist use of suicide bombers has increased dramatically in recent years. The success and glorification of suicide operatives, such as the 9/11 attackers, has been an important factor in this ideological shift.

One of the most recent suicide attacks was the Aug. 28 attempt by al Qaeda in the Arabian Peninsula (AQAP) to assassinate Saudi Prince Mohammed bin Nayef. In that attack, a suicide operative smuggled an assembled IED containing approximately one pound of high explosives from Yemen to Saudi Arabia concealed in his rectum. While in a meeting with Mohammed, the bomber placed a telephone call and the device hidden inside him detonated.

In an environment where militant operational planning has shifted toward concealed IED components, this concept of smuggling components such as explosive mixtures inside of an operative poses a daunting challenge to security personnel — especially if the components are non-metallic. It is one thing to find a quantity of C-4 explosives hidden inside a laptop that is sent through an X-ray machine; it is quite another to find that same piece of C-4 hidden inside someone's body. Even advanced body-imaging systems like the newer backscatter and millimeter wave systems being used to screen travelers for weapons are not capable of picking up explosives hidden inside a person's body. Depending on the explosive compounds used and the care taken in handling them, this method of concealment can also present serious challenges to explosive residue detectors and canine explosive detection teams. Of course, this vulnerability has always existed, but it is now highlighted by the new tactical reality. Agencies charged with airline security are going to be forced to address it just as they were previously forced to address shoe bombs and liquid explosives.

## Actors

Currently there are three different actors in the jihadist realm. The first is the core al Qaeda group headed by bin Laden and Ayman al-Zawahiri. The core al Qaeda organization has been hit hard over the past several years, and its operational ability has been greatly diminished. It has been several years since the core group has conducted a spectacular terror attack, and it has focused much of its effort on waging the ideological battle as opposed to the physical battle.

The second group of actors in the jihadist realm consists of regional al Qaeda franchise groups or allies, such as al Qaeda in the Arabian Peninsula, Jemaah Islamiyah and Lashkar-e-Taiba. These regional jihadist groups have conducted many of the most spectacular terrorist attacks in recent years, such as the November 2008 Mumbai attacks and the July 2009 Jakarta bombings.

The third group of actors is the grassroots jihadist militants, who are essentially do-it-yourself terrorist operatives. Grassroots jihadists have been involved in several plots in recent years, including suicide bomb plots in the United States and Europe.

In terms of terrorist tradecraft such as operational planning and bombmaking, the core al Qaeda operatives are the most advanced, followed by the operatives of the franchise groups. The grassroots operatives are generally far less advanced in terms of their tradecraft. However, any of these three actors are capable of constructing a device to conduct an attack against an airliner. The components required for such a device are incredibly simple — especially so in a suicide attack where no timer or remote detonator is required. The only components required for such a simple device are a main explosive charge, a detonator (improvised or otherwise) and a simple initiator such as a battery in the case of an electric detonator or a match or lighter in the case of a non-electric detonator.

The October 2005 incident in which a University of Oklahoma student was killed by a suicide device he was carrying demonstrates how it is possible for an untrained person to construct a functional IED. However, as we have seen in cases like the July 2005 attempted attacks against the London Underground and the July 2007 attempted attacks against nightclubs in London and the airport in Glasgow, grassroots operatives can also botch things due to a lack of technical bombmaking ability. Nevertheless, the fact remains that constructing IEDs is actually easier than effectively planning an attack and successfully executing it.

Getting a completed device or its components by security and onto the aircraft is a significant challenge, but as we have discussed, it is possible to devise ways to overcome that challenge. This means that the most significant weakness of any suicide-attack plan is the operative assigned to conduct the attack. Even in a plot to attack 10 or 12 aircraft, a group would need to manufacture only about 12 pounds of high explosives — about what is required for a single, small suicide device and far less than is required for a vehicle-borne explosive device. Because of this, the operatives are more of a limiting factor than the explosives themselves, as it is far more difficult to find and train 10 or 12 suicide bombers.

A successful attack requires operatives not only to be dedicated enough to initiate a suicide device without getting cold feet; they must also possess the nerve to calmly proceed through airport security checkpoints without alerting officers that they are up to something sinister. This set of tradecraft skills is referred to as demeanor, and while remaining calm under pressure and behaving normal may sound simple in theory, practicing good demeanor under the extreme pressure of a suicide operation is very difficult. Demeanor has proved to be the Achilles' heel of several terror plots, and it is not something that militant groups have spent a great deal of time teaching their operatives. Because of this, it is frequently easier to spot demeanor mistakes than it is to find well-hidden explosives.

In the end, it is impossible to keep all contraband off aircraft. Even in prison systems, where there is a far lower volume of people to screen and searches are far more invasive, corrections officials have not been able to prevent contraband from being smuggled into the system. Narcotics, cell phones and weapons do make their way through prison screening points. Like the prison example, efforts to smuggle contraband aboard aircraft can be aided by placing people inside the airline or airport staff or via bribery. These techniques are frequently used to smuggle narcotics on board aircraft.

Obviously, efforts to improve technical methods to locate IED components must not be abandoned, but the existing vulnerabilities in airport screening systems demonstrate that emphasis also needs to be placed on finding the bomber and not merely on finding the bomb. Finding the bomber will require placing a greater reliance on other methods such as checking names, conducting interviews and assigning trained security officers to watch for abnormal behavior and suspicious demeanor. It also means that the often overlooked human elements of airport security, including situational awareness, observation and intuition, need to be emphasized more than ever.